I0560713

American Expat

Moving Abroad Solo After 60

Barbara Grassey

MIND'S EYE
PUBLISHING

Mind's Eye Publishing LLC

Print ISBN: 979-8-9857928-9-8

eBook ISBN: 978-0-615-65650-2

Contents

Introduction

"I am not the same having seen the moon shine
on the other side of the world."

~Mary Anne em Radmacher

Even though living in Europe had been on my bucket list for almost my entire life, I waited until it felt like the nation and the world were on fire before making the jump overseas. Literally people were dying.

In 2020, the world was caught in a pandemic that gave us a very real view of what a dystopian future would look like: People were sick and dying from a new disease that we had no treatment for or, at the beginning, a vaccine to prevent. Businesses were closed, there were shortages of basic necessities (I'm looking at you, toilet paper!), streets were eerily empty.

No one knew what the next day would bring.

If that sounds like what you're experiencing today, this book is for you. This is the book I wish I had had when I made the decision to leave the US. In spite of the research and preparation

I did before moving to Portugal, I was incredibly unprepared for what I would face. My first year as an expat called for some quick thinking and the occasional stroke of luck. It also involved a lot more anxiety and stress than was necessary.

This book covers my decision to move to Portugal, the visa process I went through (it changes on the regular and I've added the most recent changes to the Appendix), and what it is really like to live as a local here. I had *general* knowledge of Portugal—weather, geography, a bit of the history and culture. For some reason, I thought that the US expat population was much larger than it actually is—there's about 14,000 US expats here, which is about 0.1% of the population. I chose to move to the Algarve region because it has a large tourist industry and most of the Portuguese people in the area under the age of 40 speak some English.

But there was so much I didn't know and wasn't prepared for. My transition would have been so much easier and less stressful if I had been clued in. While nothing can take the place of spending an extended period of time in the country you want to move to—and I highly recommend that people make scouting trips before moving abroad—I want to give you as much information as I can for you to make the best decisions about moving overseas for you.

Why Portugal?

I read the book *Kidnapped* at an impressionable age and I couldn't think of anything better than tramping through the Highlands of Scotland. That's where the idea started—I wanted to live in Scotland! I blame Robert Louis Stevenson. Stay with me here.

"Move to Europe and live there for at least a year" was on my bucket list since before bucket lists became a thing. I wanted to explore Europe the "right" way—not as a tourist. That item stayed on my goal list for over 30 years.

I finally went to Scotland with my mom and two of her friends in June of 2001. It was a bus tour of Ireland and Scotland, almost all senior citizens. I was a last-minute addition to the foursome; my mom's friend had fallen ill and I had a passport.

I had lived in Florida for over a decade and had become used to the climate. I had my luggage and jacket beside the door. When the airport shuttle arrived, I grabbed my suitcase and headed out. Didn't even notice my coat waving at me, saying "Hey! Wait!"

Did you know that Scotland is cold in June? Very, very cold. I learned this as soon as I stepped off the plane.

It turns out that Scotland is cold just about every month of the year. I hear August is nice. I made it through the trip with sweaters and long underwear. Considering I had spent the better part of my life searching for a warm climate to live in, I managed to enjoy it thoroughly. However, my chattering teeth made it obvious that I was not cut out to live there.

I know. I'm a wuss.

I started looking at southern Europe and decided on Italy. My father's parents were from Italy and it looked like I might be able to tap into that to get residency and possibly citizenship. (I wasn't thinking that far ahead, to be honest.) I got the language course for Italian as a practical first step. I failed miserably.

Spoiler Alert: Failing at languages will be a recurring theme in this book.

Nevertheless, the line item on my bucket list became "Move to Italy and live there for at least one year."

The Dream

As a dream, it was all far away from my everyday life. Something to look forward to in the hazy future known as someday. How do you just pick up and move countries? Sure, I wanted to experience Europe as a resident, but it was just one of those dreams people have. Crazy idea. Pipe dream.

I made up budgets: How much would I need to fly there, to rent an apartment, to keep myself in food and electricity for a year... and still travel? I was looking at $30,000 minimum. At the time, I was working as a temp, doing stand-up comedy at night, and teaching comedy traffic school classes. Let's just say that savings were thin. Okay. Nonexistent. In fact, I quit stand-up comedy (no loss to the industry) two nights before I left for Scotland. But I still taught classes and did some theater. If I was ever going to move "live in Europe" from a pipe dream to reality, I needed a new career.

Pivot

The early 2000s saw the real estate run up, not just in Florida but across the country. My parents had both been Realtors, and my father had fixed up and rented houses. I tried my hand at that and fortunately for me, any idiot could buy a property at that time and make money. I became active in investor meetings and ran one of the more successful meetings in the area. My reputation expanded and the requests to speak on real estate investing started coming in! I aligned with one of the "Old Guard" investors. We created content, shared training documentation and started holding seminars. It was the new career I needed to make the dream of travel possible. With stand-up comedy in my rearview mirror, this was a lucrative endeavor where I could use my speaking skills and expertise while doing something fun

During that heady time, my friend, Chris Krimitsos, came to me and asked if I could help him with a real estate course he had written. We re-wrote his course, added some videos and he was off and running. He said, "Barb, why don't you re-write the course from your perspective and then you can go out and speak on this, too. That way I don't have to travel as much." So, I did. Yet another skill set that would ultimately play into my dream of living abroad: Nobody does such a big thing without the collaboration of others.

Another local investor wanted help with her course, and a friend referred her to me. And then another. Pretty soon I was writing based on my own knowledge as well as ghostwriting real estate courses for speakers, including a few TV personalities. What I didn't know was that I was pricing my services way below industry norms. Some things you learn too late. I became regionally well-known in the industry and made enough to keep a roof over my head... until the crash.

And just like that, I was out of business. Broke. My Roth IRA was wiped out because the money had been invested in properties. Most of my big real estate guru clients were struggling to stay afloat. But I had a new skill—writing courses and books—and I could do it from anywhere with Wi-Fi. What at the time looked like a disaster created a full pivot into writing for an actual living—something else that had been on my bucket list for decades. It was the business that would enable me to finally make my dream of living in Europe come true and it was a solid business lesson, to boot: What looks like a grand misfortune in the moment can turn out to be exactly what you needed.

I expanded my writing to include business books and had a steady, even thriving business. Yet it was never enough to put $30,000 and a year aside to go live in Europe.

The Push

In December of 2009, I rented a nice condo on a deep-water canal in a lovely little town in Florida at a ridiculously cheap price because of the crash. I sat on one end of my couch, laptop in lap, churning out words for my clients. It is wonderful to work in a T-shirt and shorts, and not have to leave the house.

But I sat in that same place for so long, I actually wore down the leather on that part of the couch.

In 2016, my oldest brother died. We used to joke about him sitting on one end of the couch, day and night, whether there was a party going on around him or not, watching his shows. And I realized that I was sitting on the same end of my couch as he did on his. He was 65. I was hitting my late 50s. His wife had been really good about getting him out and traveling. They had gone to Europe several times. They toured all the baseball stadiums in the US. He had done a lot of things he wanted to do, but I know he would have wanted to do more. One thing about humans, we might not know exactly what we want, but we know we want more of *something*.

That was a bit of a wake-up call, but still, Italy and Europe were out of my reach financially. The way I wanted to do them at least.

The years churned on. A friend became very ill and I nursed him through two years of hospitalizations. I took an online coaching job to help with the medical bills, and that's where I met my friend Mary Anne "I'm Not Dead Yet" Radmacher. In September of 2019, Mary Anne and her handsome dog Webster moved into the condo with me. Fortunately, they were both patient while I adjusted to living with people again. And something else contributed to getting closer to realizing expat dream. On Mary Anne's first excursion to Europe decades earlier, she wrote an aphorism that has become a rallying cry for adventurers around the world, "I am not the same having seen the moon shine on the other side of the world." Her enthusiasm for travel in Europe was unmistakable and it further underscored my own.

Then, in January of 2020, COVID hit. Of course, we didn't really know much then. By March, people were dying by the hundreds, then the thousands. We were in full lockdown. My business once again came to a grinding halt while the entire world tried to adjust to this new reality.

The most important and fortuitous part? I turned 62 (ah, now we're all doing the math!) and I could collect Social Security early. With no money coming in, no vaccine, and no idea if I would live to see 65, I signed my little butt up. Not only did that decision make living through lock downs and a global pandemic easier, but it was the key that enabled me to move to Europe—a steady, reliable income.

In those 20 years between accidentally traveling to and freezing in Scotland, deciding to move to Italy and actually getting to the reality of moving, Italy changed its requirements for residency, upping the minimum income and reserves requirements. The income I had; the reserves I did not.

Just Shift a Little Bit to the Left

My friend Kellie McRae had been traveling the world as a digital nomad. She had spent time in Chile, Nicaragua, Chiang Mai Thailand, and had finally settled on the Yucatan Peninsula of Mexico. Kellie and I would talk and message endlessly about business and marketing, and always worked ourselves around to places we would like to travel to and possibly live. When I told her Italy was out of my reach, she suggested I look at Portugal. She gave me a link to a YouTube channel run by an American woman who had moved to Lisbon. One of the first videos I saw talked about the visa process and she had a downloadable checklist for the visa process that gave me my first concrete steps. She showed me the path. That initial exposure was influential in the manner in which I would become the same kind of portal and inspiration for the long-held bucket list/dreams of others.

I started doing my research. Portugal wasn't as warm as Florida in the winter, but I'm originally from New England; I can handle "mild" winters.

I met all the income requirements. I read the glossy magazine articles that talked about how affordable Portugal is (only a little bit of a fib on their part). The research pointed me to settling in the Algarve region of Portugal—the warmest part. I planned to take my scouting trip in summer of 2020 and move in 2021. Here comes another one of those obstacles I mentioned earlier.

But COVID.

Everything was shut down. Everything was in limbo. Nothing was certain. It was that exact uncertainty that persuaded me that every minute besides this one is uncertain. So, what the hell? COVID or not, I got up off my couch and stayed off it.

I decided to emigrate anyway.

Chapter One

I Understand My Decision-Making Process Seems Whack.

Choosing Portugal As My New Home

I had settled on living in Europe as an eight-year-old child. I, a grown woman, was about to pick up my life and move it overseas because of some idea that got stuck in my head before I could write in cursive. Ridiculous?

Frankly, we make a lot of great decisions as kids and then the world tells us that our dreams are stupid or impossible. But by the time I was eight or ten, I knew I wanted to be a writer and I wanted to live in Europe. Then, of course, I got mangled in the system known as "reality," not understanding that everyone's reality is different. It took a long time to figure out that much of reality is what you make it. Or what you can afford to make it, if the truth be told.

With the exception of my two-week trip to Scotland and Ireland, just about everything I knew about daily living in Europe came from watching British TV shows. So, yeah. I knew next to nothing. I did know that I would have to make cultural adjustments. Fortunately, I had lived in different regions in the States and quickly learned that people usually did things a certain way for a reason. In Hawaii, you walked on the shady side of the street. In Georgia, you hand-drew schematics because the town was too small to have official blueprints for many areas. If you ordered tea in the south, you got a glass of cold, sweet tea. If you ordered it in the north, you got a cup with a teabag in hot water.

Knowing that there would be compromises and weirdness, I started thinking about what was an absolute requirement for me (besides reliable Wi-Fi—I would still need to work) and then, what were some of the "nice to haves."

I wanted to live in a relatively warm area of Europe that I could use as a base to explore. I wanted to be close enough to an ocean to walk to the beach or even—Did I dare dream?—get a place with a water view. I admit I am spoiled—I had the good luck to live near the Gulf of Mexico for 30 years. Some places I lived actually had a bit of a water view—if you leaned out the window and tilted your head. So, I knew that wasn't an impossible dream. BUT... it seemed like a lot to ask. Even the voice inside my head that said "I want an ocean view" was a dream scaled down by reality. I really wanted to be close enough to hear the waves hitting the shore. That was another item that had been on my bucket list for years. Living *near* the water was non-negotiable. Having a water view was a nice-to-have. Hearing the waves? Tempting the wrath of the gods. **Spoiler Alert:** I got really lucky on this one.

Then I got practical.

I needed a place with a fairly low cost of living. In the expat world, there are tons of places with a low cost of living: Mexico, Ecuador, Thailand, Croatia, Turkey... Portugal's cost of living is no longer super low; it's slightly lower for me than living in Florida. And looking at Florida rents now, it's quite a bit lower. But the days of finding a two-bedroom house or apartment for €500 a month are long gone in Portugal, unless you go into extremely rural areas.

I also needed a country with a good health care system. I'm hitting that age when my body starts going haywire. I'm older, not super old and already, everything hurts for no apparent reason. What the actual---? There's a reason why old people are cranky.

Frankly, it doesn't matter how good a country's health care system is if you can't afford to access it. Most countries in Europe have some form of national health care. It's the norm. There are also parallel private systems and I knew that private health care insurance would cost much less than in the US. I checked the quality of Portugal's healthcare system: Portugal was just behind the US in health care rankings, coming in at #24 (of well-developed countries). So, it was on par.

Knowing I would have a hard time learning the language, I also needed to at least start out in an area where some of the people would speak English. Now, understand that my goal is to become fluent in Portuguese. But when I read that most Portuguese under 40 or so can speak some English (in fact, many are incredibly fluent), I felt reassured that I would be able to find someone who I could communicate with which would help my transition. I chose the Algarve because it gets a lot of English-speaking tourists (there are almost seven times as many British expats here as US) and just about every restaurant and shop will have at least one person fluent in English. If I had moved to a rural area in the interior, I would likely be unable to communicate beyond hand gestures; I'd be isolated and have an even harder time getting by.

I also needed a place with good public transportation or a central location. I knew I wasn't going to have a car when I first got there and I might never have a car there. I mean, that's the whole thing about Europe, right? Great public transportation.

I like to say my needs are small. I am sure every ex-boyfriend of mine just rolled their eyes. As it turned out, there were a few things on my must-have list that I'd overlooked. I would discover them soon enough.

Portugal checked all my boxes. It may seem like I didn't do enough research (I didn't), but my requirements were probably less demanding than most people's. Did I consider other countries? Yes, but most didn't pass the temperature test. Yes, I know that seems superficial, but I don't want to spend my golden years wrapped up in blankets. I had friends who were looking at Ecuador, Mexico, Costa Rica, Belize—all great places with a lot of US expats, but I knew I wanted to be in Europe. And most of Europe is too cold for me to live there. That narrowed things down to southern Europe. Italy was out. I had no faith in my ability to learn Greek. I have had friends in Serbia and Croatia but I still hear echoes of war when I think about those countries. I will visit all those places, but my choices really came down to Spain and Portugal. For some reason, I barely considered Spain. It may have been that the residency and citizenship process was longer.

The more I read about Portugal (and watched YouTube videos), the more it seemed like a relaxed place where people were actually happy. So, while it seems like I chose Portugal on a whim, it was already stealing my heart.

Things Get Real

Once I had decided on Portugal, and had picked out an area as my starting home base, the next step was obvious: It was time to pull the lever. It sounds simple enough, start the visa paperwork, but it feels like you are standing on the edge of a very high cliff, scary and exhilarating at the same time.

I understood it would not be a smooth ride. There would be differences in physical things (refrigerators are smaller, for instance) as well as culturally (cappuccino is frowned upon after 10:30 or so—I pay no attention to that one). I knew it was risky to move to a country that I had never been to and where I knew no one. I also knew that if it didn't work out, I could return to the States, a luxury that most immigrants don't have. In one sense, that escape plan made it easier to move ahead. But it was an option I didn't want to have to use. Paradoxically, having an out helped strengthen my resolve to make this work.

The decision was made. I was FINALLY going to go after my goal of living outside the US! It's amazing how quickly things happen once you say yes to adventure.

Chapter Two

Getting My Ducks in a Row to Move Abroad

At this point, the decision wasn't real. I knew I wanted to live in Europe and I was fairly sure I would base myself in Portugal. But, I didn't just "decide" to move. I thought I did. It turns out the decision to move was really a series of decisions, each one building on the last, yet getting more granular. I had to say yes to every step and every step made it more real.

Moving abroad is a big leap, physically and metaphorically. When you've had a dream for decades and you finally put the gears in motion to actively pursue it, it gets a little scary. Okay, it gets big scary. Scary for my friends, too.

"You're just going to pick up and leave the country?" They didn't add "Are you crazy?" I could hear it anyway.

But, as I started my preparations, I realized I had been positioning myself to make this jump for years. I would like to say that it was serendipity, but really, it was my subconscious mind slowly moving me towards my goal. I'm not one of those "meant to be" people. I like to think that I am IN CHARGE and making VERY CONSCIOUS DECISIONS!

However...

Yeah. I probably make a lot of subconscious decisions.

A lot of people right now don't have the luxury to let this decision marinate in their minds for a while. They are making very conscious, major decisions that also need to be made sooner rather than later. That's a hard reality. I will tell you upfront, that in spite of all the pictures of beaches and cobblestone streets and the many coffees in sidewalk cafés—and yes, all of that is real and as wonderful as it sounds—moving to a new country has mental and emotional challenges, just to make the practical challenges all the more... challenging.

Forget all the logistical stuff for just a minute.

Truly, the biggest issue to deal with in moving to another country is that you are leaving family and friends behind. If you are fortunate enough to be moving with a friend or your partner, at least you have each other. But I was literally flying solo.

Most of my friends are scattered across the country and my family lives in Massachusetts, so seeing most of them involved travel of some sort, whether it was driving 100 miles north to the Tampa area or getting on a plane and flying to Boston. I was already used to keeping in touch with people through phone calls, texts, emails, and Zoom. But Portugal is 4,000 miles away. An ocean apart. Wrapping my head around that was a little tough.

The pandemic and quarantine actually made it a little easier to leave—I couldn't visit with most of my friends and family anyway. And I wouldn't be able to in the foreseeable future. I know many, many people in the US are contemplating leaving because they no longer feel safe. They don't like the direction the country is headed in. And not everyone can move.

But for most people, I think leaving the love and safety net of friends and family has to be the hardest part of moving away.

Emotions aside, I was fairly well set up to make the big move.

The work part was covered. As I said, I had nothing anchoring me to the States; I could work from anywhere. I had no parents or kids or romantic entanglements. I'm not dissin' on my lovely gentleman friend who I had been in a long-distance relationship with for half a dozen years. But, while it was pleasant and fun, it had pretty much run its course for both of us. I had sold all my real estate back in the crash and I've been a happy renter for years. (Much better than being a landlord; not as good as being a homeowner in some respects.) My lease was up at the end of November 2020. I didn't have a pet or plants. In short, there was nothing tying me to one location.

As I mentioned in the Introduction (you DID read the Introduction, yeah?) the pandemic pushed me to apply for my Social Security benefits early and in so doing, removed the biggest obstacle to moving overseas. You need to show steady, reliable income or enough money in reserves to immigrate. That holds for just about every country. I'm self-employed. A one-gal shop. Which means my income can be up and down and most years it rings in at about the same amount, but it comes in chunks, not a set weekly paycheck.

Of the countries I looked into, Portugal has one of the lower income thresholds for immigration. While I can't live on my Social Security benefit alone (yes, even in Portugal), the monthly payment is more than enough to qualify for the D7 passive income visa.

So, I would still need to work—even while living in Portugal.

I've been in my current business for about 20 years, which gives me a lot of credibility when government agencies look skeptically at the ticked "self-employed" box. I had a dedicated home office, but, when I wasn't meeting with clients, I was sitting on the couch with my laptop, cranking away. I had deliberately built a business that allowed me to work from anywhere just in the hopes of one day moving abroad. So even before COVID, I conducted 95% of my business via the Internet. In truth, I can work with all of my clients remotely; it just happened that a few of them were local to me in Florida. I was confident that my clients would be fine working with me longer-distance. As long as I had a Wi-Fi connection and electricity, I could conduct business.

I also knew that people didn't have a problem hiring me remotely. When I was first in business, I thought it would be a bigger problem than it was. I started as a ghostwriter and added nonfiction book coaching. Both involve substantial deposits. Who would send some woman they had met on the Internet thousands of dollars? (I mean, outside of lonely men?)

Since over 90% of my clients are personal referrals, there is a certain amount of trust built in. I meet with people to discuss their needs and wants in a free consultation which helps them get to know me and know that I am a legitimate business. I was worried that might change if I moved to Portugal.

As it turned out, no. In fact, people seem more eager to work with me because—get this—they think I'm cool. (Shh. Don't tell them.) They like to see what the weather is like when we have our sessions and will often ask what is going on here or what Europe thinks of what's happening in the US. I'm still waiting for some of my US clients to come over and see Portugal for themselves.

And Some Cons

But living overseas came with some very real drawbacks for my business. Because I coach people, I need to meet with them at a time that is reasonably convenient for both them and me. The five-hour time gap between Portugal and the US East Coast is fairly easy to work with. The additional three hours to the West Coast created a little more of a challenge. For the most part, it means that I would stay available until 7:00 pm Portugal time a couple of nights a week. Not a huge sacrifice. And while I still count time zones on my fingers when manually setting an appointment with a client, my scheduling software does that for me. I now send people to my scheduler to book an appointment. The scheduler knows my hours and converts them automatically to the time zone my client is in.

I would also lose out on in-person speaking engagements that helped me raise my visibility and bring in clients. In the midst of the COVID crisis, speaking engagements had disappeared and event promoters were just figuring out how to do live, large-scale events online. Until the pandemic was over, it didn't matter where I was living; live speaking engagements weren't in the cards.

My finances weren't precarious living in the US. I could make money. If worse came to worse, I could physically go get a job. I had skills, a solid reputation, and a network. If I moved to Portugal, I would have none of these things.

Moving to a new country, even a new state, on a shoestring budget puts you at a disadvantage. In this real world, money solves a lot of problems. Not having "extra" money, a buffer, makes everything harder. It limits your options. At the very least, you have to be more flexible and resourceful.

Part of my evaluation process was calculating the risk, not of losing business, but not being able to attract as much new business as I needed. I knew that I needed to build in a financial buffer for at least the first year of living in Portugal.

I'd Been Here Before

I sat my medium-size butt down and evaluated the pros and cons. Just because I could do this didn't mean I should do it. When I thought about it, I realized that I had made major moves before. I moved from Massachusetts to Georgia to Florida, back to Georgia, to San Francisco, then Hawaii and back to Florida.

As I made my final evaluations on moving to Portugal, I thought back to my most complex move: San Francisco to Hawaii, way back in 1989. Moving to Portugal had a lot of similarities to that move. I had never been to Hawaii and I only knew one person there. But I knew I wanted to live in Hawaii. It had been on my goal list for almost a decade.

Then I remembered how I financed it. Or in truth, how I didn't have the finances to make the move. If I had a better grasp of reality at the time, I probably wouldn't have made the jump. I prepaid for a week in a hotel in Waikiki with the idea that I would find a cheap place to live—which I did. I may have had $2,500 cash reserves in total after shipping belongings via a cargo container, airline ticket (one way), and the hotel. I had the (maybe) promise of a job and when my money started getting low, I signed on with a temp agency. The job came through about five months later. I didn't starve. I didn't die. I had a lot of fun.

Older and wiser, I had a much better grasp on reality this time around. As I worked my way through creating a real budget, I felt more confident about making the move.

The Deciding Factor

The pieces falling into place, all the calculations and spreadsheets and research are important, but they are logical. All left-brain stuff.

What was the deciding factor? What overcame my inertia? Mortality. I am getting older and less mobile. At 62, I wasn't old or frail, but another ten years of sitting on the couch would sideline me. Making the leap was a do it now or never do it at all situation.

Mostly I just got mad because I had spent decades lying to myself. I gave myself a thorough chewing out: *How can you say you want to do this but not do it? Either you really want to move to Europe or you need to take it off the bucket list and never go.* Basically, I kicked my own ass.

There was nothing stopping me from finally living in Europe. It was time to either make the leap or stop yapping about it.

And then I got another push.

Chapter Three

The Short Hop

At the end of May 2020, my landlords sent an email saying they were putting the condo on the market. My housemate, Mary Anne, and I started looking at options. She had already been exploring moving to a university town. I figured I would go back to the Tampa area. We had no desire to be living in a condo that was on the market—having people trooping through, having to get out of the house for any showings or open houses, doing five-minute pick-ups on short notice. We asked the landlords if it would be helpful for us to move out early and yes, of course it was. Suddenly, our move-out date went from November 30th to July 31st.

Mary Anne had completed a major cross country move a year before, which brought her to Florida. She had less stuff and better muscle memory of moving. I, however, had been living in the condo for ten years and had accumulated a lot of STUFF. Much of that stuff I had accumulated over a lifetime and had merely added to.

My cousin has a condo north of Tampa that sat empty most of the year. She kindly rented it to me at a rate that barely covered her utilities and condo fees. My goal was to get rid of as much stuff as possible before moving to her condo so I would have less to deal with when I finally made the big move.

You know, ya think you're really getting rid of stuff. You're donating to the charity shops, throwing things out. You're being "brutal" about those sentimental items... but my books! I can't get rid of my BOOKS!

Books are heavy. Just sayin'.

I donated what I thought was a lot of books but I still ended up with cases of books.

Mary Anne found the perfect place in June in a university town and had been week-ending up there, taking small loads of things with each trip. But two months is not a long time when it comes to packing and moving. We were both scrambling to pack all our things and get out of the condo by August 1st.

I have moved many times in my life and I feel pretty confident of my packing skills. I once packed up an entire house in 24 hours after getting off a red-eye flight from Vegas. But that had been almost 20 years before. I had more stuff and less stamina.

I do know enough to bite the bullet and buy moving boxes. And lots of tape. Going around to grocery and liquor stores, collecting boxes to use that may or may not have had something weird in them just doesn't cut it when you are in a hurry. Small boxes for the heavy stuff, large for the light stuff, and definitely,

definitely, wardrobe boxes for your closet if you're using a moving company.

Unfortunately, we were not using a moving company. The hanger stuff got grouped together in amounts we could lift and covered with a big trash bag. Mary Anne rented a van for two days (and drove it—I'm a wuss when it comes to driving big vehicles; she is fearless). Anything we deemed too big for the cars went in the van. We did several trips up and down I-75. My cousin's condo was about the halfway point between Punta Gorda and Gainesville (albeit a thirty-minute drive west), so we'd load Mary Anne's stuff first, then my stuff. We'd offload my stuff at the condo and Mary Anne would continue on to Gainesville.

At various points, I hit overwhelm and Mary Anne, staunch friend that she is, put up with my temper tantrums, meltdowns, and indecision, and got us both out of the Punta Gorda condo. Little did she know it was a practice run for getting me to Portugal.

Our legs were sore from going up and down the stairs. Our arms and shoulders (and heads) ached. We totally overstepped using the condo's shared trash bins. Even with twice-a-week collection, they were constantly full. The real estate agent was eager to get the condo on the market and she kept telling us not to worry about leaving anything—she'd take care of it. When we mentioned we were getting a cleaning company in to make sure the place was left in good shape, she said she had a company and we were happy to hand her the cash. When we took one last sweep of the condo, I looked at the odd assortment of things being left behind: I was leaving behind my glass L-shaped desk, and file cabinets (the agent said she could use them), foam floor tiles for working out, stacked neatly, the odd assortment of cleaners

We made our final trip up I-75 and settled into our new places. My cousin's condo was filled with boxes I would need to go through, this time with an eye to what would come with me to Portugal and what would go in storage. I set up my "office" on the dining room table so I could still work. I took a week to settle in, sort myself out, and rest.

There was no more avoiding it. It was time to figure out the visa process for Portugal.

Chapter Four

The Visa Process

Who Could See That Chapter Title Coming?

I had traveled out of the US a few times in my life: I had been to Ireland and Scotland as a tourist, which didn't require any visas. I had worked on a small cruise ship in Mexico and a bigger one that sailed the Caribbean. As a purser, I had dealt with customs and immigration officials in the various countries. But as a US citizen and a crew member, I didn't have to deal with getting my own visa. The only visa I had ever applied for was done for me by the company I worked for—a visa for Bahrain at the start of the first Gulf War. Fortunately, that one was never used. (A story for another day, perhaps.)

When I got down to it, I had no understanding of the visa process for emigrating to a new country. My YouTube guru, "Driven Spice," pointed me to VFS Global, the company that handles and checks all the visa paperwork before it is submitted to the Portuguese Embassy. I downloaded a fresh checklist of requirements (they change frequently) from their website and immediately felt overwhelmed.

My passport needed to have six months of time left on it when I arrived in Portugal. I had about a year left—my passport would expire in August of 2021. I wanted to renew my passport so I would have plenty of time on it, but we were in COVID lockdowns. Passport offices were closed for all but emergencies. Eventually, they would start to reopen on a limited basis, but getting your passport renewed could take anywhere from four to six months or, hey, it could fall into a black hole. I checked to see if any of the same-day passport offices were open. I looked at driving up to Atlanta but I didn't qualify as an *emergency* situation. I decided I would get my passport renewed once I arrived in Portugal—which meant getting my butt to Portugal as soon as I could.

As I read down the checklist, it felt like getting the visa would be a mountainous task. Thanks to Driven Spice's videos, I knew I needed a D-7 visa for people with passive income, so I was saved that bit of confusion. The D-7 also allows you to earn money, but the main requirement is being able to show enough passive income to meet Portugal's requirements. Thank you early Social Security.

I decided to tackle the list one thing at a time. Can I tell you? It's the only way I could do it. Otherwise, I would have just melted into a big ball of overwhelm. I'm a fairly competent person and I know that eventually, I will figure things out. But with the uncertainties of COVID, moving out of my apartment of ten years, and making, really, a pretty huge decision, my overwhelm meter had been pegged in the red for months.

The next thing I did was download the application form. It was, of course, in Portuguese. Enter Google translate. Some of the things were easy: name, address, age, citizenship. But wait, why are they asking about residency? Oh, some US citizens don't live in the US—they are residents of other countries. Like what you're about to do, Barbara!

Then I found a copy of the form in English! Well, that's easier. I filled out the parts of the form I understood and left the rest for further research. Ex/National Identity Number if applicable. I'm an overthinker. *Do they want my Social Security number? No. That can't be. Passport number? No, they ask for that below.* The US doesn't have a National Identity Number. But that's the type of thing I would leave blank and get back to when I could face it.

If you're wondering, the application form was all of three pages (the fourth was blank). It wasn't that complex. But, as glad as I was about finally making the move to Europe, I was freaked out as hell. It took very little to push me into overwhelm. Knowing this, I decided to do as much as I could and when things got too hard (i.e., I didn't understand what they were asking), switch to something else. Sometimes your brain just gets tired. If you come back to it fresh, you have more energy and "Oh! Yeah! That's what they want." Once I had the English form filled out, I just transferred my answers to the Portuguese language form.

The part of the process that takes the longest is the FBI background check, so I decided to work on that next. Now, I don't care how good a person you are, the idea of asking the FBI for a background check just seems like asking for trouble. It's like going into an IRS office and saying, "Hey, I pay my taxes but I'm just checking to see if I owe you any *more* money."

All those times I stole (and ate—is that destroying evidence?) a little two-cent Peppermint Patty when I worked the Woolworth's check-out flashed through my mind. Well, what did they expect putting me that close to chocolate for hours at a time?

I decided that the statute of limitations had run out on the candy. I went through the FBI process and got the special code number I needed to set up the fingerprint appointment. I followed the online instructions to set up an appointment with the closest post office that did electronic fingerprinting—the Orlando office. The online booking system didn't work. I tried calling. No one picked up. This went on for over a week and finally I resigned myself to driving to Orlando (about two hours) to make the appointment, and then make a second trip.

I printed out the directions for the trip to Orlando (yes, I am that old!), found the specific post office and joined the other masked patrons on line. There was a special window for passports and fingerprinting and lucky me, there was a family of seven doing their passport applications. SEVEN. Who has five kids in this day and age?? Fortunately, they had already been there a while. When I finally got to the window, the clerk was a sweetie. Or maybe he was just happy that I didn't have an entourage to check through. I asked to make an appointment to have my fingerprints done. No need for an appointment—he could do them now. Yay! No second trip!

He started the fingerprint process.

And that's when I found out that old people's fingerprints wear off.

What? I could have been leading a life of crime for the past few years?

Try as he may, he could not get my fingerprints to show clearly. If I couldn't be fingerprinted, I couldn't get the FBI background check. If I couldn't get the background check, I couldn't get the visa. If I couldn't get the visa... NO!

My face must have shown the absolute panic I was going through.

The clerk smiled at me. "Don't worry."

He reached down below the counter and brought out a bottle of Corn Husker's Oil. He had me rub it on my fingertips.

Success, for the most part. (One of my fingers still wasn't quite clear.)

With that done, he just needed my code number to send the prints to FBI headquarters. I needed to go back on the FBI website and get *that* number.

Something you need to know about me: I am really not good with phones. I am a total boomer when it comes to phones. Half the time when I try to answer my phone I hang up on the caller. I do NOT surf the web on my phone. I do not do banking on my phone.

But I needed that number.

I sat in my car, trying desperately to get Wi-Fi and not really understanding how the whole data plan/Wi-Fithing works. I mean, don't you need to hook onto someone's Wi-Fi? I was not successful. I would have to drive somewhere and find Wi-Fi, or more likely, since I can't do anything on my phone, I would have to find an Internet café or library and use their computers. And, oh yeah, COVID lockdowns. Not a whole lot of places were open.

I put the phone down and opened up my file folder. I looked at what I had printed out from the FBI. And there, on the page, was a number that *looked* like the number I needed. I put my mask back on and went back inside.

"You mean this number?"

"That's it!"

And just like that, my fingerprints were zooming off to Washington, DC. Now all I had to do was wait for the report to be mailed to me and remember not to open the sealed envelope.

One-half of one step accomplished.

What could I do next?

I needed to have six months of accommodations set up. I had planned to take a scouting trip in the summer of 2020 to get a feel for the country and see where I might want to live. Humans make plans and God laughs. That trip, of course, had turned into a quick move out of my condo and making the big leap blind. I had no concept of the geography of the country, outside of the fact that the Algarve was in the warmer south. Should I throw a dart and hope for the best?

In one of the Facebook expat groups, people mentioned that they had stayed in Airbnbs and used that as their six months of accommodations. (For the record, this is no longer the case.) I hit the Airbnb website, but I still didn't know anything about the places I was looking at. I got out a map and decided somewhere near the center of the Algarve would be a good starting point. Albufeira kept coming up as a tourist destination so I started looking there. I quickly found out that when you rent an Airbnb for over a month, the price goes down by about half. That really helped keep me within my budget.

But what if I set up for six months in one place and hated it? Also, I wanted to check out other cities before I decided where I would live permanently. I decided to book three separate apartments for two months at a time. (My time working on ships taught me that I can do anything for four months; two months would be a cakewalk).

Then the big question hit: How long would it take to get my visa?

That depended on when the FBI report came back. And after that, the processing time with VFS and the Portuguese Embassy could be anywhere from three to six weeks. It was October. I was waiting for the FBI report. If I got everything in by mid-November, I could move in January.

I would move to Portugal in January. It was happening.

I booked the three Airbnbs, two in the tourist town of Albufeira and one in a town called Nazaré, way up north. I don't know why I chose that; maybe I had heard about the huge waves that brought world-class surfers there. (FYI: I do not surf.) Most likely it was because I had no idea where it was—I figured it was on the western coast kind of near Lisbon. Geographically, Portugal is about two-thirds the size of Florida. How far could it be? Turns out it's another hour and a half north of Lisbon. If you have a car.

I paid for the first month of each rental, and would be billed for the second month as each came up. Great! I was only out three months' rent instead of paying all six months up front. That was helpful.

With the accommodations set up, I booked my flight. I was set to fly out on Monday, January 4, 2021. I tried not to think about what would happen if my visa didn't come through on time—or at all.

The FBI package came back and really, wouldn't you just want to know what the FBI has on you? I managed to resist opening the envelope—I figured if the FBI had a dossier on me, my visa wouldn't be approved. I would have to trust that I had gotten away with the Peppermint Patty pilfering.

I had printed out so many copies of things that my printer ran out of ink. No problem—order more ink, right?

No.

Along with toilet paper, printer ink (and I imagine copier ink) was in short supply. I tried ordering online, the big box office stores, even places like Walmart and Target. No one had the right ink cartridges. I ended up buying a cheap printer because it came with ink. Ridiculous, but I was on a mission!

I assembled the visa package for VFS. I wrote a short, three-paragraph essay on why I wanted to move to Portugal. I figured out the weird questions on the application. I had the FBI file. I signed the form giving the Portuguese government permission to check my criminal record in Portugal. (No sweating that one.) And all I needed was a certified copy of my passport. Something that doesn't exist, or perhaps it was just a bad translation of what they wanted that didn't exist.

I made two color copies of my passport and went down to my local Amscot to get it notarized.

"We can't notarize that."

"You're just notarizing that it's a legitimate copy of my passport. Here's my passport, here's the copy. Look."

"We can't notarize that."

Are you kidding me?

I went back online, trying to figure out what a certified copy of my passport would be and where I could get one. No luck. I decided to see if a different notary would do it. (Really, I was hoping to get one who wasn't bright enough to know they couldn't notarize a copy of a passport.) I called a notary a few towns over, asked if she could do it.

"Sure. No problem."

We made an appointment for the next day and she notarized it in the garage of her house, with the garage door open. We both wore masks.

I took my two notarized copies, paid the lady and left. If there was going to be a problem, I figured VFS would let me know.

Lesson Learned: Just because one person or company can't do something doesn't mean nobody can. It turns out that the Amscot notaries are very limited in what they are allowed to notarize. So are bank employees. If you get a "no" from one place, go to the next. And the next.

I made copies of EVERYTHING, got the whole package together with a money order for VFS, and sent it off. It was close to mid-November.

I received an email letting me know the package had been received. Then a couple of weeks later, a second email arrived, asking me to FedEx my passport along with two separate money orders for the return FedEx and embassy fees.

And three days later, my passport was returned to me with the visa stamped in it. Smooth as silk. In less than a month, I'd be leaving for Portugal.

I was really going.

Gulp.

Chapter Five

But... COVID!

Last-Minute Details

Even though I had spent the past several months organizing paperwork, sifting and sorting, throwing out even MORE stuff, and donating, I still had lots of last-minute details to handle: transfer car titles and registrations, talk to the insurance company and cancel my insurances, find out if I could use my phone in Portugal, and oh yeah, pack up everything that *wasn't* coming to Portugal with me. Since I was only taking two suitcases and my computer bag, that meant most of the possessions I had left. I found the smallest, least expensive storage space that would work, five feet by five feet, with the idea that if something didn't fit, it would go into the trash or to the charity shop.

I am a hoarder of paper: old scripts, manuscripts (half-finished), letters and mementos, playbills from college, etc., on top of things like real estate closing papers (two big boxes) and past taxes. (I know the IRS says you only have to keep them for seven years, but I don't trust 'em.)

On top of that, I still had kitchen and barware, shoes (and shoes and shoes!), large pieces of artwork (those I took off the four by five foot frames and rolled) and framed artwork, a flatscreen TV, clothing. Anything that I couldn't fit into those two suitcases would be put in storage until I had a permanent place. My life—and my cousin's condo—was filled with Rubbermaid storage tubs.

I needed to sell my car, a '98 Audi convertible, a classic with a perfect body disguising a myriad of costly headaches. The tricky part was I also needed to have a car up until a day or so before my flight. I was saved by my cousin's significant other, Gary. He offered to buy it. I explained over and over to him that the car was a money pit, but he is extremely good-natured and likes a project. Can't say I didn't warn ya, Gary. As problematic as that Audi was, I had loved that car and I was happy to see it go to a good home with someone who would love it, warts and all.

The holidays had a bit of a melancholy tinge to them since I was experiencing perhaps my last Christmas in the States. Once again, my friend Mary Anne swooped in to help me sort and pack. She stayed with me at the condo for the holidays and our Second Annual Christmas Harry Potter marathon. We had started the "tradition" the year before with a three-day Harry Potter marathon, cupcakes, cinnamon rolls, eggnog, and well, generally behaving like little kids who have been allowed to design their own holiday. There was a lingering sense that we may never get to do this again, so we went all out. She had brought Webster, the most polite dog in the world with her. I love this little guy and he had grown to tolerate me with a minimum of side-eye. Though every so often, when I would do something goofy, he'd just give me that look.

New and Improved COVID! Yay?

The week between Christmas and New Year was a week of uncertainty. Another strain of COVID had been found and countries were shutting borders again. Brexit was not helping—with the UK pulling out of the European Union, I didn't know if EU countries were allowing flights from England to land. My scheduled flight connected through Heathrow. A person on one of my Portugal Facebook groups said her flight had been canceled. Someone else said they were rerouted through Amsterdam. I didn't know if this was temporary or the new way of doing things.

Another person said that only citizens and residents were being allowed into Portugal. I had a residency visa—did that mean I could enter? Or did I need some other, more finalized paperwork? It was dawning on me how much I didn't know about how *anything* worked. I just had to hope that I could get it all figured out in the three and a half months before my in-country residency appointment. That was, if I could get in the country at all.

I made a conscious decision to act as if things were going to work out just fine and I plowed on with that thought. Then, as now, I couldn't control what was going on in the world and, outside of checking with the embassy in DC after the holiday, there wasn't much I could do. My only choice was to keep moving forward as planned.

No matter where you move, things are constantly changing: forms change, requirements change. Throw in COVID and all the health considerations involved when you allow people to enter your country, temporarily or permanently, and you can understand why things were so uncertain. I was left to hope that the availability of vaccines would ease things a bit. But it was early days. Vaccinations had just started on December 14th, and they were reserved for the most at-risk among us.

In those last few weeks, I made rounds of telephone and Zoom goodbyes with friends because... COVID. I wished I could give people good, hard hugs but that would have to wait until we could visit in person again. I wondered if this would be the last time I saw some of my friends. I tried not to dwell on the answer.

So, I took a deep breath and looked ahead.

Moving Forward

Pro Tip: If you think you have tossed and donated as much as you possibly can, let me assure you that you still have too much stuff.

As I said, my final week was spent still sorting, tossing, and packing. Mary Anne kept me moving--basically lighting a fire under my butt. My goal was to get everything—all my possessions—down to eight bins and a guitar case.

NOT EVEN CLOSE. I had four bins of books that I had packed and brought to storage, feeling quite saintly that I had done "ALL THAT" before Mary Anne arrived.

We packed and made trips to the storage place and to the local Goodwill store. I am lucky that I know how to pack for long trips so deciding what to bring for clothes was fairly easy. When I first worked on ships, I had a rotation of four months on, two months off. Packing for four months is the same as packing for two weeks. I reminded myself they have washing machines in Portugal. The trick would be not to over pack and throw my back out before I got the luggage to the plane.

I took bags to the dumpsters at night so people wouldn't see me filling them up. And in between, we had coffee and cake and delicious take-out from the nearby Greek place. We knew that our time together was closing out soon and I think we both wanted to savor those days.

We packed right up to the day before I left. The final count? (Best sung to the tune of *The 12 Days of Christmas*):

- 7 big blue Rubbermaid bins

- 6 slightly smaller bins

- 5 contractor bags holding 9 vacuum storage bags of clothing and linens

- 4 boxes/wrapped bags of artwork and a TV

- 1 tube of rolled artwork (the Lost Ertés, as I call them)

- And a guitar case sitting on top.

All of it skillfully Tetrissed into my five by five foot storage unit by Mary Anne. (She has mad skills.)

My Favorite Part of this Process: Using those vacuum storage bags.

Correction: My Favorite Part of this Process: Watching Mary Anne throw herself on the bag containing my oversized comforter to squeeze all the air out like she was throwing herself on a grenade.

We made final decisions about what to take and what to leave. Everything had to fit into my new suitcase and carry-on. We used packing cubes and the whole thing looked very organized and orderly. You know I wasn't in charge of that, right?

So, what was I thinking on the eve of leaving the US for my new country?

To say that I wasn't scared would be a flat-out lie. I was scared and anxious and excited and I am sure my eyes were wide with both fear and anticipation. Was I making a huge mistake? That was a possibility that didn't bother me—worse came to worse, I could move back to the States. That's a back-up plan that most immigrants don't have.

I don't know what made me want to leave behind everything I have ever known. But, I'd done it before. For a while, it seemed

I moved every five years. I moved across the country from Atlanta to San Francisco. Then I moved from San Francisco to Honolulu. This was a bigger jump, and possibly a permanent one. I just get itchy feet.

I am reminded of a comment my fourth-grade teacher put on my report card: "Barbara excels in class, but she doesn't really pay attention." Or something like that. (I didn't pay too much attention to that, either.) To be fair, my desk was near the windows that faced the courtyard. I could see people walking down a corridor, other classrooms, birds and squirrels in the courtyard. So much going on and I was trapped in a square room. I guess I don't like feeling trapped anywhere. That and there was so much going on outside that box. There's a whole planet to explore. I understand that not everybody has the means or opportunity or even desire to explore it. But me? I had no excuses. It was time to fly.

Chapter Six

The Adventure Begins!

Monday, January 4th, was my departure date. I was flying American Airlines to Chicago, and then British Air to Heathrow, Heathrow to Faro, Portugal. (For the record, I didn't know how to pronounce Faro at the time.)

Mary Anne delivered me to the airport by 1:00 pm; my flight was leaving at 4:00. I waited in line at American for 20 minutes, wrestling my big suitcase, carry-on, and my computer bag. I got to the very nice ticketing lady who said, "You can't go to Portugal; the borders are closed." I was 62 years old. I knew how to lead with confidence, i.e., BS someone. I drew myself up to my full five foot five, and assured her I could enter Portugal because I had a residency visa. She looked through my passport, examined the visa and nodded. (I have also learned not to look surprised when someone believes me.) COVID test? Check. UK Passenger Locator Health Form? Check. Portugal Health

Form? Uh, what? She showed me where to get it online. I tried to do it on my phone. Did I mention I can barely answer my phone? Fifteen minutes of watching me try, bless her. I went down to one end of the American counter and opened up my laptop. Bam. Got it! I am unstoppable on a laptop.

During all this, I could hear the ticketing agents talking: "Trying to get all the flights out by 4:00 pm. They're shutting down the Jacksonville Air Traffic Control office. Don't know why." They're not telling the passengers this. I had just been standing at the counter for so long that I pieced it together. My flight was at 4:00 pm exactly. I felt a small knot of panic forming in my stomach.

My agent finished the ticketing process. She charged me $75 for the bag, a fee I was pretty sure I had already paid online. Grrrr. And an extra $100 for the bag being overweight. Well, that's cheaper than shipping stuff to Portugal. I told her I would straighten out the fees later, paid the $175 and headed to the gate.

I settled into a seat at the gate area, prepared to make a few phone calls to finish up some business when I heard my flight being called. *Early*. Way early. They weren't kidding about getting everyone out before Jacksonville shut down. But wait! I forgot to find the currency exchange, I had no euros and I didn't have enough cash on me. More important, I hadn't gone to the bathroom yet! Oh well, the first leg was a short two-hour flight, I can wait.

Because the flight was full, they asked people to gate-check their carry-ons. "You just pick it up at the gate when you get off the plane." Cool. I did the gate check with my small suitcase that had paperwork, works in progress, client notes, and a few books. I kept my laptop bag with all the really important paperwork, i.e, copies of my visa paperwork. Still, gate check was a **BIG MISTAKE.**

The gate agents and flight attendants were trying to get everyone on board and seated so they could push back from the gate early and get us in the air. The plane was PACKED. No empty middle seats on American. We were handed little Ziploc baggies with a sanitizer wipe, a small bottle of water, and my treasured Biscoff cookies (my FAVORITE part of any flight). I turned my face to the window and considered double-masking.

Flight attendants did the crosscheck. Cabin lights dimmed for takeoff and...

The Adventure Stopped.

Nope. Sorry.

We all trooped *off* the plane. We were told we'd be delayed anywhere from three to five hours. Or maybe just one hour. They didn't know. It didn't take a whole lot of calculating to figure out I would miss my connection to Heathrow in Chicago. I checked email and found that American had already anticipated this. I called the 800 number the American email had told me to call because my flight needed to be changed. It was no longer in service. Seriously. The recording gave me another number. I called that and talked to a very sympathetic woman who could not help me.

"There are no flights to Portugal until next Sunday."

"I am very sure there are flights," I explained to her. "Planes fly there every day."

"Well, no flights on our partner airlines," she said.

"So, stick me on another airline. You sold me a ticket to get me to Portugal; you need to fulfill your part of the bargain."

We booted it up to a supervisor. I explained to him that everything I owned was in a five-by-five storage space or on his plane: I have left my condo, I have sold my car. I had no place to go. (A bit of a fib.) Am I supposed to live in the airport? If so, will they put me up at the Airport Marriott? Um. No. He was also polite, but useless to me.

All the time that I'd been on the phone, I had also been standing in line at the gate. I finally made it to the front and the gate lady was WONDERFUL, but we couldn't get my gate-checked bag back. She sent me downstairs to the American ticketing counter to see if they could retrieve it.

This may come as a surprise to you, but there was a *very* long line there. Full of *very* unhappy people. I shuffled in line, as one does. The person behind me had no concept of what six feet looked like. We were ten months into this pandemic and people still weren't distancing. I put my computer bag between us to keep a little distance. There was a soldier on leave a few people behind me. She was humping two huge duffels and a backpack.

My shoulders and arms were aching from my stupid computer bag. I was in awe of her.

I finally made it to a ticket agent. My earlier agent saw me and called over, "My Portugal lady!" It's nice to be recognized. I'm pretty sure it was the hat I was wearing.

We put in a request to get my luggage off the plane. At this point, the plane was re-scheduled to depart at 6:20 or so, but I had spent so much time getting off the plane, then standing in two separate lines, that they couldn't guarantee they could get my bags off the plane in time. We looked at rescheduling my flight. Friday at the earliest but wait, no thank you: There's a 24-hour layover in Heathrow. *Não é bom.* Not good.

I trudged down to the luggage center. Another very nice agent. She said there was a chance—very small—that they would get my luggage off the plane, but it was close. And it could take an hour or more to get to her office. I told her, "I can wait. I'm going nowhere."

I hadn't eaten since breakfast and I was trying not to be cranky. I hadn't been drinking as much water as I should have been. I was tired and disappointed and truly, wanted to cry. I waited. I walked over to the luggage office and looked at the luggage that was there, hoping my shiny new suitcases were among them. From time to time there was a line of people at the office coinciding with each canceled flight. One man yelled at the lady. I had talked to him in the gate line. He was recovering from a car accident, got hit by a drunk driver. Broken pelvis, broken legs. He was expecting a big settlement check. He told me it hurts to stand and to walk. He may be an asshole, but I understand he is an asshole in a lot of pain. He was young and didn't yet know that he will hurt for the rest of his life. He didn't know that even a big settlement check doesn't make up for a life of pain. I felt bad for the lady; I felt bad for him. My personal bad was somewhere in between the two.

I sat, trying to figure out my next move. After an hour or so of hope, I talked to the luggage lady, Donna. No joy. She promised to check on it in the morning, and took down my number. She said with so many flights being canceled, I probably wouldn't see my luggage back in Tampa until Thursday at the earliest. Good news: It won't go all the way through to Portugal. It won't leave the States. And neither, apparently will I.

SECOND MISTAKE: I didn't get a number for her office. I expected to be shuffling through voice mail systems all day Tuesday trying to contact her.

Stranded. Sort Of.

I had to get back to my cousin's condo and cab fares were running around $100 plus tip. That's a decent bottle of scotch. And the scotch will last a LOT longer. Priorities. The Super Shuttle service closed down years ago, I was informed. I tried the Uber app. I figured it would be good practice for when I am carless in Portugal. The app kept spinning and loading when I typed in my pick-up location and desired destination. I tried it over and over again, thinking I would get a different result. Duh.

All this time, I had been texting with Mary Anne. She was running her mastermind group but offered to drive down after 9:00 pm to get me. A ridiculously long drive, over two hours, especially at night. But she would do that because that is the kind of person she is. I considered my options. I knew a lot of people in the Tampa area but who can you call at 8:00 pm to drive 40 minutes north and then home again? When you reach a certain age (ahem), most of your friends have trouble seeing at night.

I called my friend Chris Krimitsos of Podfest fame. He was perfect. Lives near the airport, his parents live near where I've been staying so he knows the way, and he's younger so he can see at night. (A very attractive attribute in Florida.) I got his voice mail. Crap. I sent him a text and thought about who else might rescue me. Chris called me back a minute later. "Where are you? I'll come get you." WOW.

He knew the fastest route to my cousin's condo. We chatted and caught up on the half hour ride. I offered money for gas/time. He refused. Then he told me if I needed a lift back to the airport, to give him a call and he drove off into the night. That's a friend.

I walked back into the condo. Turned on the lights, water heater, water. Reset the thermostat. Grabbed my car keys and headed to Target. I was focused on coffee, cream, and underwear. Literally, every pair of underwear I owned (except for what I had on, thank you), was in my luggage. (Because I *gate-checked* my carry-on. Did I mention that was a *huge* mistake?)

It was ten pm, I was tired and unfocused. I realized I needed something to sleep in so I added a man's T-shirt to the cart. I looked for "soft pants" like sweats or shorts that I could wear around the house. I couldn't come to a decision. I had enough brainpower to pick up a toothbrush, thinking ruefully about the two new toothbrushes in my luggage.

Back at the condo, I was too tired for a drink even though I could have definitely used one. I boiled up some angel hair pasta, added butter and parmesan and let it go at that. I numbly watched two episodes of NCIS because that was all I could handle doing. I headed to bed on the nice clean sheets that I had left for my cousin to come back to. They felt good.

Tomorrow Is Another Day, Scarlett.

It will all get handled. Tomorrow.

I usually say that I "slept the sleep of the innocent" when I have a good night's sleep. That night I slept the sleep of the exhausted. Physically, emotionally, mentally. It's a big psychological jump to leave your home country for someplace new. I had to stop Mary Anne several times during the packing and tossing and loading phase because it was suddenly too big and overwhelming. All my stuff going into storage. Leaving everybody and everything I knew. Not knowing the language or how to get from the airport to the Airbnb, or even whether or not I would be allowed into Portugal when I got there. With COVID, things shifted daily.

So, I slept deep and long and the next day I had a headache and residual unrest. I drank my Peets' coffee, took some (more) Ibuprofen, and got to work on making new arrangements. On the plus side, I now had a little more time to tie up loose ends from here rather than trying to do it from Portugal. And, on the incredibly lucky side, I discovered that the UK had locked down all outgoing flights. I could have been stuck in Chicago (very cold). Or I could have been stuck in Heathrow. Either way, I wouldn't have made it to Faro. Silver linings.

I was disappointed beyond belief. But for the time being, more coffee. There was lots of work to do. I had always said that I could work from anywhere with my laptop, Wi-Fi, and coffee. And I can. I was determined to get the train back on track. Because really, what could possibly happen on a weekday in early January that would distract me?

Chapter Seven

What a Week to Be in the States!

In the words of the great George Takei, "Oh my."

The biggest items on my agenda on the morning of Tuesday, January 5th, 2021 were finding my luggage and adjusting to my disappointment. I like to wallow in self-pity as much as the next person, but hearing that Heathrow had been shut down made me feel a little better about my flight getting canceled. Not much, but a bit.

In addition to finding my luggage, I had to secure new flights. I ended up rebooking the same flights, just one week later. This time I got smart and, on the insistence of a friend's mom, booked a driver to pick me up in Faro and drive me to my first Airbnb.

I spent a lot of time on the American Airlines phone tree, trying to find my luggage. I called the national number, talked to the national baggage lady. She called the Tampa luggage office. She started with, "I have a passenger who was going to Port ugal..." and the Tampa lady said, "Barbara Grassey! I have her number right here." So, Donna in Tampa totally had my back. American was still trying to sort things out because, and this will shock you, closing down air traffic control for the entire southeastern part of the country really screws up... everything. In the business, I believe that is referred to as a Charlie Foxtrot.

Best guess: My luggage was definitely NOT leaving the country and my bags were "probably" sitting in Chicago. *Great*, I thought. *Because no one steals anything in Chicago.*

I sat back to assess my situation and started making a new to-do list. I'd have to get another COVID test, but I couldn't do that until Friday. I needed food for the week. I now had time to get euros. I made a few phone calls to straighten out some car insurance issues. Mostly I tried not to think about baggage handlers in Chicago rifling through my stuff and laughing at my granny panties. I was not successful.

I went out to get groceries and comfort food. Cookies always make me feel better. I also picked up a few more clothing items. I tried to get euros at my bank but really, trying to get euros in Pasco County, Florida is a fool's errand. I figured I could get them on Friday when I went down to the airport for my COVID test.

I talked with Mary Anne and my cousin. I skimmed Facebook, responding to people who asked if I was in Portugal. That would be a nope. I ended up writing a blog post just so I wouldn't have to explain what happened over and over again. Scrolling through, I came across an interesting little tidbit: Someone had breached the air traffic control communications system at JFK Airport the day before, threatening to fly a plane into the Capital building on Wednesday. Authorities deemed the threat noncredible and were much more concerned that the communications system had been breached. Maybe Monday was just not a good day to be flying anywhere.

I had a slightly better dinner than the night before and watched some TV, feeling depressed. *I had been sitting on the plane!* So close.

I went to bed fairly early Tuesday night, exhausted. I felt like I had accomplished next to nothing. I decided to give myself a little grace because I had done what I could—most of what I needed was out of my control. Mary Anne's poem about courage came back to me. *"I will try again tomorrow."*

I slept late on Wednesday and did not feel the least bit guilty about it. I made my coffee and did my usual walking into walls until the coffee kicked in. Showered. Started a small load of laundry because I had only a few items of clothing. There would be many small loads this week. I checked in and updated Facebook. I texted and talked with friends. I put in another call to American Airlines' national line to see if my luggage had been located. Basically, putzed around, as we say.

And then Facebook lit up like a Christmas tree.

I flipped on the TV and was glued to the events unfolding at the Capital. We watched in disbelief and then horror as the

Capital was breached. Why weren't the usual crowd control checks in place? In spite of rioters breaching the perimeter barriers, lawmakers walked into the House chamber to count the electoral vote. Vice President Mike Pence tweeted that he could not determine which votes should be counted or not counted; he was constrained by Constitutional law. He hadn't told the White House about this prepared statement in advance. Tweeting it put his life in danger, but I suspect he knew it was already in danger. Damned if he did, damned if he didn't. I've never been a fan of Mike Pence, but I respect what he did that day. Ten minutes after Congress assembled, Trump ended his speech by urging his supporters to march to the Capital building.

What followed were hours of absolute craziness: brutal and graphic scenes. My friends and I were messaging back and forth on Facebook, adding in events and rumors and trying to stay as informed as possible. No one knew how the day would end. Hours later, reinforcements finally mobilized (in spite of intentional chain-of-command delays). Some had arrived and more were on the way. They turned the tide. It was evident that the insurrectionists would not be successful, Trump released a video telling "protesters" to go home, while still claiming he had won the election.

By 8:00 pm, the Capital building was once again secure. Lawmakers reentered the trashed Capital building and with Vice President Mike Pence presiding, continued the count of electoral ballots. They stayed in session all night, finally finishing the count at 9:40 am on January 7th.

People were dead. Many more injured. In the following days, a flurry of pointless, CYA resignations from White House officials were submitted. Other resignations were called for.

And we were all pretty much shell-shocked by the events.

Friends congratulated me on my decision to move to Portugal. But my decision wasn't at all political. I just wanted to experience Europe. After the events of January 6th, I was feeling better about my decision to leave the country.

Now, people are making the decision to leave the country based on very real political dangers. No one can say that Trump isn't following through on his campaign promises. (Well, except anything that would actually benefit the average American.) He promised to be a dictator on Day One and he followed through. He is targeting anyone he perceives as an enemy or an "other." While I would like to think that people are moving to Portugal and other countries because they want to live there specifically, I fully understand that for many, they just need to leave the United States and leave it fast.

The violence of the day and really, the violence that was part of the "normal" course of life in the States—mass shootings, and school shootings in particular—was something I didn't want to live with. I lived in Florida which had an "open carry" policy. It was always unsettling to walk into a Starbucks or a Walmart and see people with guns on their hips. I mean, really, are you going to have to fight someone to get your soy mocha latte?

I was glad to be almost out of it.

Over the next few days, more and more stories came to light, creating a timeline of events that dated back to before the election.

Friday rolled around and I needed to take a COVID test for my Sunday flight. I did my usual putzing around, thinking the testing center was open until 3:30.

I checked the Tampa Airport testing center around 12:40 and discovered to my horror that it closed at 1:30, not 3:30. I lived 45 minutes away. I grabbed my wallet and keys and broke land speed records. As I got out of my car in the airport parking garage, I realized I had forgotten a mask. There were none in the car. I asked a lady walking by, "Do you have an extra mask? I forgot mine!" I couldn't go into the airport without one. CRAP!

She didn't, but she said the information desk had masks available. I rushed into the elevator and hit the button for the third floor. I got out and checked the line for the test—I had eight minutes. I was holding my jacket up to my face, covering my mouth and nose, and a security guard pointed me to the information desk. I was apologizing to people all over the place. The lady at the desk gave me a mask and I joined the line for testing. There were three other people behind me when they cut off the line. Phew!

Once again, I tested negative for COVID. I was cleared to fly. I stopped back at the information desk to ask where the currency exchange was. No currency exchange in the airport. I'd be flying to Europe without any euros. I sighed, but in the grand scheme of things, not a major issue. I'd get euros when I got there.

I also stopped by to see Donna in the luggage office. She recognized me immediately, brought out her clipboard, and showed me that she had checked on my bags three times. She must have called again before she left for the weekend. I got a call a few hours later from Tania, telling me my bags had been located and would be on my flights with me, available for pickup in Faro. I thought, *I'll believe it when I see it,* but really, why not? The tag team of Donna in Tampa and Tania in Chicago had come through for me! Now I just had to hope that my possessions were still in my bags... As it was, I was reconciled to losing all my possessions, even though the paperwork in my small suitcase was irreplaceable. I asked myself, "What would you do if it had all burned up in a fire?" Somehow that helped me over the anticipated loss.

I drove home at a more sedate pace, determined not to let anyone breathe on me before I got on the plane. Now I only had three worries: If the flight would actually take off; if I could transit through Heathrow; and whether or not I'd be turned back once I reached Portugal.

Sunday morning, I changed the sheets and did a couple of loads of laundry. I packed my new clothing acquisitions in a Nantucket bag and repacked my computer bag. (There may or may not have been an extra bag of Peet's Major Dickason's coffee in there.) I shut off the water, unplugged the car battery so it wouldn't drain while it sat for a few months, made sure the condo was secure. Chris Krimitsos came through for me again, picking me up at the condo and delivering me to Tampa International.

Second time's a charm?

Chapter Eight

BSing My Way into a Country

BSing Does Not Get the Credit It Deserves.

And... we're in the air.

This time around in Tampa, my paperwork was organized and ready to go. No questions asked. The first leg of the trip was packed again—no empty middle seats. It was NOT a comfortable feeling. I turned my masked face to the window and tried not to breathe deeply. This was a domestic flight and at least half the passengers hadn't been tested for COVID. I strongly suspected they were the ones who wore their masks under their noses. I was nervous about the virus; I could not begin to imagine the level of anxiety airline personnel and public-facing people must have felt on a daily basis.

I was also worried about connecting in Chicago. O'Hare is huge and my connection time wasn't. As it turned out, the gate I needed was just a short walk away. I had time to hit the Dunkin Donuts (*my last Dunkies* sighed my internal monologue) and grab a hot chocolate and a bagel. I ate the bagel in short bursts, replacing my mask as I chewed.

My flight was called and I was happy to see that it was obviously not a full flight. Someone from immigration had the happy task of taking each passenger's picture as they came down the gateway, asking us to pull down our masks to get the shot, and then wishing us a good flight. I settled into my row, happy that there was no one else in it. In fact, most of the rows only had one passenger. Or none.

I was flying the same route as I had set for last Monday when Jacksonville Air Traffic Control shut down. I was right—second time is the charm, but I didn't feel like I was really leaving until I boarded the plane in Chicago. I wondered if my luggage had been put on the plane with me and decided I had no control over it. I would find out when I got to Faro.

Chicago to Heathrow is about a four-thousand mile flight. We had a tailwind that varied between 40 and 60 MPH and an airspeed of 560 mph. The outside temp was -65.2 degrees which was, I thought idly, cold enough to keep the Pfizer vaccine stable. A bit too chilly for this Florida girl. Over the next few hours, I watched it go down to -81. I didn't know it was an omen.

I was too keyed up to sleep which meant I had lots of time to think. The past week in the US had been nothing short of a shit show. (I mean, really, the POTUS put out a *HIT* on his own VP. Mike Pence must still be wrapping his head around that one and I don't blame him. I am no Pence fan, but sheesh, that's a bit extreme.)

I felt like I was finally starting my new life. And, if something horrible happened before it all started, at least I wasn't sitting on the same corner of that same damn couch. As the plane took off, I had a strange thought: "Escape from the US."

We were fed—something that may have been chicken parmesan with an orzo mix. I meticulously picked out the bits of broccoli. So much for "new year, new me." The cabin had been darkened. I know the technique. The crew wants us all to sleep which will make the trip faster for everyone. I'm good with that. Back when I worked on ships, we gave our passengers Dramamine for seasickness. It would put them right out. They were better off and so were we.

I did my best to make the crew happy and tried to stretch out across the seats to take a nap. I can't remember the last time I had an entire row to myself. That doesn't happen very often anymore so I tried to take advantage. I put the blanket over me and wedged the pillow between the armrest and the bulkhead, tucking up my legs so they wouldn't hang in the aisle. It was not comfortable. Airplane sleep is never solid. I didn't show it on the outside, but I was way too excited to sleep. I sat back up and watched our progress on the screen, seeing places under the North Atlantic I'd never heard of: Charlie-Gibbs Fracture Zone, Eirik Ridge, Immarsuak Sea-Channel... What places will

I miss out on because they exist beyond what I once thought was a well-rounded education? Starting over.

We landed in Heathrow and all but one terminal was shut down. I didn't see any airline or security people and I had no idea where I was supposed to go. It was definitely eerie—the only people in this huge area were my fellow passengers. I decided to follow the people getting off my plane, an advanced technique that made it very easy for me to find the proper connections area. Sometimes it's better to be lucky than good.

I checked in with British Airways. The ticket agent, in his clipped, official accent, told me I can't get into Portugal; it's closed. I squashed the urge to say, "So is England, but here I am!" No, I pointed out politely and with false confidence, I have a residency visa. I live there. (Well, technically not yet, but...) He called a supervisor on the phone and we played 20 questions:

Do I know anyone there? (No.) Do I have accommodations set up? (Yes, six months.) What do I do for a living? This one is a trap. I told him I'm in publishing. Freelance writers are seen to be as economically viable as hobos and carnies, so I gave him a respectable and close enough answer. Do I have a business card? (Of course!) The business card seems to give me some credibility. I don't know why—it's the one I use for events and it's colorful and salesy. But printed on good, thick stock.

I showed him a letter from Portuguese immigration that says I have a residency appointment scheduled for April. "I have to be in Portugal for this appointment, don't I?" It clinched the deal. They decided I can go and the agent, who had been polite all along, apologized. I had done three months of paperwork, crossed all the Ts and dotted all the damn Is and I still felt like I was bullshitting my way into a country.

I found a currency exchange and ask for euros. The man explained that we have to put my US dollars into British pounds and then convert to euros. "This is very expensive," he told me. "You're losing money on both exchanges. Just do a little bit for what you need and do a larger exchange when you get to Portugal." I am touched by his kindness.

I got a mix of euros and pounds and wandered off to find coffee. I had a few hours until my flight. I got in line at the first kiosk I saw. There were lots of people in the terminal, but that was probably because it was the only terminal open. The coffee I got was horrible; muddy, lukewarm, bitter. I sat with it for a few minutes, trying to swallow it, but really, it was a no-go. I was shaky with lack of sleep, caffeine-deficit, and fear.

In spite of my earlier show of confidence with the British Airways agent, I was terrified that I would be turned back at Faro Airport. I wasn't sure how I would handle that. Where would I go? Would they let me stay overnight and then put me on the next plane back?

I wandered some more, and everything seemed a bit of a blur. I spotted a Starbucks not too far from the first kiosk. I am not a fan but I knew the coffee would be strong. I got an over-priced large coffee (not a vente, thank you) and some sort of cheese toastie, and sat at a table to eat. It restored me a bit. Then, I headed off to find my gate.

Another fairly empty flight and we took off on time. This was it. I was actually going to Portugal! I prayed that I would see more of it than Faro Airport.

In Faro, I once again followed the other passengers and got in one of the lines for customs and immigration. All the lines were short, but some people took longer than others. I shifted over a lane so I would be the last one in that line. I figured my processing was going to take a while and I didn't want to hold anyone up. I also didn't want any witnesses in case they decide to throw me out of the country.

The agent looked at my passport and visa. He asked in charmingly accented English, "You live here?" I answered, "This is my first time, but yes. I am applying for residency." He said, "You just got a good president, why are you leaving now?" and we laughed. We talked about how crazy the last week was in the US and how good it was that Trump was leaving. The world had been holding its collective breath, too. He waved me through with a "Welcome to Portugal" and I was in. Just like that.

I was very sure my luggage would not be waiting for me. I followed the immigration agent's directions to the baggage claim just outside the door and... There's my luggage! Both pieces, just waiting for me! I collected them and tried to arrange at least one of my carry-ons on top of a suitcase, and unsteadily wheeled towards the exit.

Faro is a smallish airport, and I still managed to turn the wrong way after collecting my bags. I attempted to call my driver but my phone didn't work. A security person told me I was in the wrong area and sent me in the right direction. There were very few people in the area he sent me. Fortunately, one of those people was my driver, David, who did a much better job of finding me than I did finding him.

The One Smart Thing I Did

Moving is a major life transition and one that makes the top ten list of anxiety triggers. Now imagine that instead of moving to a new town or new state, you're leaving your home country. Feel a slight uptick in blood pressure? Welcome to the expat life.

It's downright scary moving to a new country and frankly, I don't think people talk about this enough. You have just walked away from everything you know (and possibly own), leaving behind family and friends and a way of life to start a new life where you are going to have to learn new things every day, from finding groceries, to driving rules (if you're not from Boston, roundabouts can be treacherous!), healthcare system... well, everything.

But the first thing is getting off that airplane and getting to your new place, whether it's a rented apartment, temporary hotel or Airbnb, or a house that you bought and haven't yet lived in.

The very, very best thing that I did (and I thank my friend's mom for her advice and worry) is hired a driver to pick me up at the airport and take me to my Airbnb. DO THIS! Get a driver. Make sure there's enough room for you and all your luggage.

Do not say, "Oh, I can get a taxi or an Uber," "I'll rent a car at the airport," or worse, take the bus or train. Yes, of course you can. But you're not going to be in any shape to deal with that. You can take the bus or train once you know your way around and you're not carrying all your earthly goods with you.

You've just been in airports and on planes for the better part of 24 hours. (Some a little more; some a little less.) You haven't really slept. You've eaten over-priced, poorly prepared airport food. You're dehydrated even if you've been drinking water. In short, you're tired and disoriented. And if you're anything like me, more than a little cranky. The more luggage you brought, the more likely that something won't show up. It will be found. Maybe not right away, but eventually.

David handled the big bag (62.5 pounds, sorry David!) and I schlepped the others. I'm going to make a huge generalization here, but I'm not going to be wrong by much: The drivers who pick you up at the airports are awesome. They look at your huge stack of luggage and your bedraggled selves and your pets and kids and then volunteer to take a selfie with you. (The airport arrival selfie is HUGE in the expat groups. I don't know why; it's just a thing.) Then they load up you and your luggage and take you to your new digs.

David's English was perfect and we chatted on the 45 minute or so drive. He pointed out landmarks along the way. The football stadium (real football, not American football) that was built for the Euro 2004 championship games. Old Town Albufeira for the "older folks." He showed me where "the kids" hang out.

Before taking me to my Airbnb, he stopped to show me "the best view of Albufeira" which is a park by the cemetery. The sun was slanting low across the water and lights were coming on, twinkling in the distance. The view was postcard magical. We soaked it in for a few minutes. Then he banged a U-Turn and took me back a few blocks. He had told me at the airport that the address I had been given for my Airbnb was not strictly an address; more of a general area. I felt panic rising up in my gut.

"We'll see if we can find it," he said easily. It would be a shared task.

We pulled into the street and the apartment building was right there. (It's barely a street.) We laughed at our success and he humped my heavy suitcase up two and a half flights of stairs. I was tired, shaky, and cold. I couldn't get the lockbox to work. He did it for me. I couldn't get the key to work. He did it for me. We hustled my bags in and I tipped him well. The big suitcase alone would have done me in.

The place was cute, exactly as pictured and... freezing. A window in the bathroom had blown open and all the cold air had settled in. There was a heater in the bathroom. I pulled the cord; nothing happened. I looked for a thermostat. Nothing. (So American of me, I know.) I messaged the owner, asking if the unit had heat. He responded that there was a heater in the bathroom (thanks, Bub) and a space heater in the closet. I found it and it became my best friend. But I couldn't get warm. I shivered and shivered. I hate the cold.

I was tired, cold, hungry, and scared. I had some leftover airline food but no means of getting a meal that night. I opened my cases—everything was intact. A miracle. I explored the small apartment, found the refrigerator (in the hall closet) and the microwave (in the cabinet under the stove top). There were teabags in the bottom drawer. I pulled out the electric kettle to boil water. It had a six-inch cord. Every outlet in the place was at least eight inches above a flat surface. Fun. I boiled a cup of water in the microwave and poured that into a second cup with the tea bag. I realized that I would be cooking for the next two months the same way I cooked in a college dorm room. Unfortunately, there was no vending machine filled with M&Ms and Suzy Qs on the next floor.

I had tea. I munched on an airline fig bar and some almonds. I went online and let people know I had arrived and I was safe. I found my fuzzy socks. I decided it would all get sorted in the morning. The TV stand had little cubbies, one with a few books. The only one in English was *A Casual Vacancy* by JK Rowling. I climbed into bed in pajama bottoms and a shirt and my sweatshirt and my fuzzy socks because—did I mention it was fecking freezing? I started drifting off as I read, so I made sure the space heater was off before I settled in for the night. Shouldn't burn the place down on the first night. Pretty sure that's bad manners.

I woke up every hour for the first three hours, with leg and foot cramps, shivering with cold. Then I went down for the count. Five hours of solid sleep.

Everything did look better in the morning, but it was still bloody cold. I opened the blackout curtains and the sun streamed in, helping to warm the place. Mr. Space Heater was cranking. Unless it was directly facing me, it didn't seem to do much so I kept it directly in front of me, not more than three feet away, not caring if that gave me wuss status. I had nothing to prove.

I made more tea and came to terms with the fact that I needed to take a shower, even if the bathroom felt like Iceland. I skipped washing my hair since I had no shampoo. I stood under the hot water until I could feel my feet and toes again. I steamed up the bathroom, hoping it would take some of the chill out of the air. Close enough.

It was my first day in Portugal. I decided to explore the neighborhood and try to find a grocery store to get supplies. And maybe a cup of real coffee. That was my entire agenda. I was keeping my to-do list intentionally short for the first few weeks. One day, one thing.

But I did it! I was in Portugal. I had a roof over my head. I had my stuff. I wouldn't freeze to death—probably. I was good with that.

Chapter Nine

It's All Uphill

Albufeira: Portuguese for Everything Is Uphill.

I had been in Albufeira for a week. I had found the closest market and I was living on ham and cheese sandwiches, Oreos, and Ruffles potato chips. I found a coffee maker at the grocery store on my first day and I at least had my precious Peet's coffee to start my day. I was using milk because I couldn't figure out cream. In fact, I wasn't even sure if I was getting whole milk or not. I decided the milk containers with the blue accent color were probably low-fat. The other choice was green. I went with it. It was whole milk! #WINNING!

Finding cream for my coffee went from a mere item on the grocery list to a side quest. There were little plastic containers of some sort of supposed-to-be-cream substance. I didn't like the product or the fact that I needed to use three little plastic containers to turn my coffee a murky brown. I actually tried crème fraiche because, how bad can it be? Bad. *Não é bom*, as we say.

I also made a new rule for myself: Don't walk downhill until I know for certain I won't have to walk farther uphill.

Some neuron in my brain fired one night during my first week and I remembered that I was supposed to register my presence with the local authorities. I logged into two expat groups on Facebook and searched to see if anyone had posted about the process but couldn't find anything. So, I asked.

Once posted, I had immediate responses, which gave me a hint as to how helpful expats were going to be in my future. (Thank you!) The replies were not completely straightforward, partially because everyone's situation was different. One said my Airbnb host was supposed to register me. One said her lawyer had told her she definitely had to register with SEF, the Portuguese Immigration and Border Patrol Services. One said she had had to register and had done so at the local Junta de Freguesia, sort of like a Parish Council. I contacted my Airbnb host and he said that he had registered me. I thanked him, but I wanted to make sure I did everything properly here, so I set off to find the Junta or Council. (Trust, but verify.)

My phone didn't work here, at least not all the time, or maybe certain functions worked, and I had no idea why something worked when it did. I didn't have GPS, or maybe I did and just didn't know how to get it to work here. I looked up directions on my laptop to get a general idea of where the place was, but I couldn't print it out—no printer.

I took a picture of the screen with my phone camera. I wasn't sure how helpful it would be because Google doesn't show the street names of the little back streets until you zoom in incredibly close and then you can't figure out where the heck you are in the big picture. And most of Albufeira is little back streets.

I set out on my quest to make sure I was street legal. The morning was fresh and warm—low 60s Fahrenheit. My brain hadn't converted to Celsius yet. But it was perfect walking weather. I masked up and walked down, down, down to the beach area, checked on the currency exchange office (closed), and tried to figure out how to pass through the warren of streets to get to the other side. Not all roads go across. They all, however, seem to go **UP**.

I eventually found myself near the main drag in town. I finally saw the McDonalds (no thank you) and the municipal building. I knew I was close. I checked the picture of the map, trying to figure out just where the Council offices were. A young man suggested I ask at the police station: "They are very helpful." I flashed on the way many people felt about the police in the States. The young man's attitude wasn't just refreshing, it was encouraging.

The policeman at the door asked my nationality then sent me to other offices in the next building over. They found a lady who spoke English and she came to the door. Very few people were actually being allowed inside buildings at this point. If business could be conducted in the fresh air fairly quickly, all the better.

She started to give me directions. I said, "Wait. Let me guess. It's uphill?" She laughed.

Another ten minutes of walking and I found the offices. In my short time here, one of the things I have learned to do is to not stop too soon. I walked farther than I thought I had to and then saw the grocery store, Pingo Doce, that the woman had mentioned as a landmark. I turned up the next street, saw the bank she told me about, but I couldn't find the offices. So, I kept going. Up, of course. It was another block, but there it sat. Two women were standing outside, distanced. I asked the first, "Are you waiting?" She indicated no and waved me in front of her towards the door. I asked the next, and yes, she was waiting. Someone will come to the door, she said, for the next in line.

We waited in the sun, maybe ten minutes. I sneezed and quickly said, "NOT COVID!" The women laughed. A popular joke in every language, apparently. A woman came out and talked to both of us. I told her what I need to do. She explained that if I am staying at a hotel—or Airbnb—the host would register me; I was all set. To me, it wasn't a wasted trip; I wanted to make sure I did everything properly. I needed the reassurance she gave. I walked away, satisfied.

I turned to walk downhill, then remembered the supermarket, Lidl, was somewhere near where I was, relatively speaking, and might be uphill. Okay. Odds were *REALLY GOOD* that it was uphill. So, I walked uphill some more and came to a soccer stadium. I walked and walked, but now it was mostly flat or slightly downhill. I found the "high rent" district: big beautiful houses behind electric gates set at the top of the city. Amazing views.

I have a pretty good sense of direction and I kept working my way around and to the left, keeping the city on my left side. I knew eventually I would come to the street that the Lidl is on.

If You're Waiting for a Sign

One of the things I really liked about Albufeira (and this is true of most cities in Portugal) is they have road signs for shops and hotels. I saw the sign for Lidl, 250m. Quite frankly at this point I was hot and a bit sweaty (a nice change from shivering, so that's not a complaint). I was tired and my knee and hip joints ached. My feet hurt. My back hurt. I had stopped my twice-a-week workouts almost a year before, due to COVID. They were always light on cardio anyway. Albufeira was helping me make up for all the cardio workouts I skipped. If my trainer knew, he'd be laughing his ass off at me.

I limped into the market and picked up a few things. I found a set of paring knives, not quite what I was looking for, but better than what was supplied at the Airbnb, which was half a dozen butter knives and one large, dull serrated knife. I looked for cream for my coffee. No luck. I was mostly checking out what they offered. I found prepped cheese and bacon burritos. BACON! Well, I did say I would try the local food...

I loaded my few groceries into my Trader Joe's bag (don't leave home without it) and decided to take a different return route than the one I knew. This led me back into the rabbit warren of streets in town. I recognized stores and restaurants from my earlier trek. The restaurants were closed, of course. Most of the shops were closed. Only the farmácias and mini-marts were open. I checked the currency exchange again. Still closed. I stopped into a farmácia to see if they sold scissors. No. That's okay. Today I got knives, one thing off my list.

I sat on a bench and ate half a croissant. I had had only coffee and yogurt so far that day and I was not that hungry, but I was also aware that if I didn't eat something, there was a good chance I would have a dizzy spell. Hundreds of pigeons and gulls live in this area, but NONE of them swooped in to steal my food, or gathered at my feet begging. I remembered restaurants at US beaches stringing monofilament fishing line to keep the birds from stealing patrons' food and the posted signs saying the restaurant would not be responsible if a bird stole your dinner. The birds here are much more civilized. Or maybe it was just a fluke.

Baby Steps

I established a very precise agenda for these first few weeks: Every day I tried to see a new area, find one thing on my "still need" list. Every day I tried to accomplish just one thing. This day, I took care of the registration question, found knives (where does Portugal sell hangers, darn it?), and explored the Lidl. I walked over 15,000 steps. There were days back in my condo that I walked fewer than 1,500.

I trudged home, saw the time and freaked out. I had a Zoom business meeting at 1:00 Eastern and I panicked—thinking I had missed it. I opened up the Zoom room and no one was there. I looked at the clock on my laptop which runs on New York time and saw that I was an hour early. I breathed a sigh of relief.

I took two Aleves and microwaved the burrito. It was yummy. No matter how tired I was and how much I ached, this day definitely counted as a win.

Chapter Ten

Setting Up My Routines

Work Still Needs to Be Done. Sigh.

I like being five hours ahead of the US east coast. I can do a day's worth of work—or play—and still take care of business. For the most part, I *don't*... but I *could*.

I was still working out the timing on some meetings. 8:00 pm EST is 1:00 am here. Evening meetings were not going to work and that was okay. It would force me to limit my appointment hours, putting them into an afternoon time block which meant my mornings were cleared for productivity. Which also meant that it was time to start setting routines.

Mostly, I needed to start getting up at a proper time. Before I left the US, I was going to bed around 1:00 am and I do that here. Well, maybe 2:00. I was waking up around 8:00 or 8:30 which makes sense as far as hours slept.

But it was cold out there beyond the covers and I usually rolled over and went back to sleep until 9:00, sometimes 9:30 and once or twice until 10:00. This was new: Usually once I am awake, I am up. I had allowed myself a week of slacking to get used to the time difference, but it had been a month now. I was still sleeping in. Avoidance. That's probably a bad sign—isolation, depression. Being a scaredy-cat about facing another day of everything being new and unknown.

But this day, for maybe the first time, I was out of bed by 8:00 am. It was cold outside the covers but not as cold as it had been. I sipped my coffee, looking out over the rooftops of Albufeira at the gorgeous beach. Sunrise was at 7:25, but the sun hadn't yet broken through the grey. The day was misty and overcast. It was eerie and lovely at the same time.

I was in a perfect spot for writing. I told myself this because it was my brain's way of pointing out that I had no excuses—this is where the rubber meets the road. If I can't get my work done here, I'm just plain lazy. (Anyone else give themselves lovely little pep talks like this?)

There was this whole Pandemic Productivity Guilt (PPG) going on. My friends (mostly entrepreneurs) and I discussed it. I don't know if it was an American thing or not. We were in the middle of a pandemic feeling guilty because we haven't used the time to learn a new language, write the Great American Novel, build six-pack abs, *and* sew a designer wardrobe. We weren't doing all those things we always said we would do if we only had time. (But I think most of us got through the sourdough bread thing fairly fast, am I right?) It was a fair bet that most of our houses weren't spotless and our offices were still disorganized. And we felt guilty because, really, this shit should have been done by now. (Says who?)

Self-Starting/Stalling

I work from home. There's no office to go to and no manager checking to see if I clocked in. I have been self-employed for 20 years. I am a self-starter. I have lived for years without an alarm. I normally wake up between 6:30 and 7:00 am. I have my coffee, walk into walls, have more coffee, make my list for the day, start work at 9:00. Miracle Mornings do not happen in my house and I'm good with that. But now, in Portugal, too often I didn't start working until noon or 1:00. I couldn't be good with that.

It might have been a bit of COVID fog. Lockdown in Portugal seemed more strict than lockdown in the States. Mostly I think the Portuguese are more considerate of each other and they were taking all those inconvenient precautions that Americans rebelled against. Most of the shops were closed; the few restaurants that were open were takeaway and delivery only. Travel between districts was restricted. Most days I wasn't going anywhere so there was no hurry to shower and dress. I suspect I made trips to the grocery store just to make sure I had a reason to shower and dress. The days had already achieved a certain sameness. I needed to use this lag time to set my routines, knowing that those routines would be a bit different here.

Time Realities

Some things just take longer here. Most of the apartments (and so, Airbnbs) don't have clothes dryers. This unit had a fantastic washing machine (15 different wash cycles–it's the F-35 fighter of Washer World), but only a small portable drying rack. I learned to hang sheets (one at a time) and towels over the railing on sunny days, otherwise they just don't dry. I'm pretty sure the wind dried them more than the sun, and that was fine. But it was time consuming. The neighbor below me hung out his laundry almost daily. His spot had no sun. Not much wind either. He almost always had the laundry hung out before I was up. I was impressed by his consistency, but now I'm sure it's a habit that was born of necessity, not industriousness.

Note to self: He had a routine. And shit got done.

My kitchen consisted of a two-burner stove and a microwave. Cooking is not one of my talents, to put it kindly. I was eating a lot of sandwiches (the bread here is fantastic!) and cooking up "real" dinners maybe a couple of times a week. I had yet to eat a vegetable here. When I first arrived, I spent a lot of time figuring out meals and groceries, trying to find foods I liked. I am not a foodie. I am not an adventurous eater. I grew up on Wonder bread and Twinkies and Welch's Grape Jelly and really, my diet hasn't expanded much since then. I'd found the major grocery stores in town and assembled a decent supply of staples. The past week, in addition to the normal bread, milk, eggs, Oreos, I picked up lettuce, a bag of frozen mixed vegetables and a couple of apples. There were vegetables in my near future. (I was in no hurry.) The cooking and eating routines were starting to normalize.

But this all takes more time than it did back in the States. I make several small shopping trips a week rather than one big trip. I didn't have a car so I chose which store I walked to depending on how much time I had available. The small one was a five-minute walk down the hill (and a ten-minute walk back up) and the bigger stores were a half hour hike each way. The walking makes shopping a daylight activity. I hand-carried the groceries back in my two Trader Joe's bags, so I'm limited as to how much I can buy at one time. I could probably take cabs or Ubers back and forth but it was an expense I didn't need to incur at this point. I also didn't know if taxis and Ubers were available and even if they were, I didn't have any way to call them. Fortunately, I felt good about walking—afterwards. Not so much during. My huffing and puffing told me that I needed to do more walking. It might be the only healthy thing I did. More Pandemic Guilt.

The refrigerators here are small compared to the typical fridge in a US house. If you ever wonder why America has an obesity problem, start with the size of our refrigerators. Though I noticed the smaller refrigerator wasn't magically taking the pounds off me, so maybe not.

When I lived in Redington Beach, Florida, I would wake up about 6:30 or 7:00 and walk the beach first thing. I think I would like to do that here. In fact, before I arrived, I pictured myself walking the beach, a cup of coffee in my hand. (My hair blowing artfully in the breeze...in slow motion... I am also a lot thinner in that vision.) But mornings were a little too chilly for me. And all the little coffee vendors were closed down. So, I told myself it would become a part of my routine when it warmed up a bit. I didn't know if I was lying to myself. It was another thing to discover.

Do What I Can

In the meantime, I needed to firmly establish my two-hour writing block in the morning to go with my not-bad-but-not-great coffee. (I did NOT bring nearly enough Peet's coffee.) I was working on putting out two blog posts and a newsletter a week. That was the hard quota. In addition to that, I had client work, regularly scheduled meetings, and several books in process. I needed to create the marketing systems for the books I had written.

So, lots to do inside when we were limited as to how far we could go outside.

And yet...

I was spending an inordinate amount of time on Websudoku and Facebook, instead of writing. Plus, the time I spent feeling guilty, of course.

But on this day, one month in, I was up. I was writing. I was getting shit done. Maybe not in the exact time frame I would have liked, but it was a step in the right direction. I would do my best to repeat the process the next day and the next. I was retraining my brain and my body, acclimating to the five-hour time difference and a new way of life. I decided I would do what I could, when I could, the best I could. And screw the Pandemic Productivity Guilt.

Chapter Eleven

Little Victories

I woke up to the sound of gulls jabbering. A thick, muffling fog had rolled in overnight. The construction on the building in front of me hadn't started yet. It's much better to wake up to the sound of gulls than jackhammers. Motivating, even.

It was cold again, but still warmer than a month ago. A cold front had moved in a week before, bringing rain and cloudy days. The country had been tamped down by COVID protocols. This day, the fog burned off revealing bright sunshine. Albufeira looked positively glorious. People were definitely ready for a break. I felt an energy that hadn't been there before. The sun was shining. The air was warm. People were out walking the streets and the beach, almost all of them masked even when walking outside. In my previous travels, I had passed little restaurants that were closed. On this Saturday, many of them were open for takeaway.

The government released pandemic figures every day, telling people what was going on in the battle against COVID. Portugal was the #1 hot spot for COVID after the Christmas holidays. Hospitals reached the breaking point and some non-COVID patients were airlifted to other countries. Medical teams came in from other EU countries. Four weeks of hard lockdown turned the tide. The prior week, WHO reported that new COVID cases were down 56.5% in Portugal, the largest decrease in Europe. Hospitalizations continued to fall. All good news. The lockdown had been extended through March 15th, but people could see that it was working and most (not all) were supportive.

All of this kept me from exploring as much as I like. Or maybe it gave me an excuse not to explore. When I thought of going out, which meant downhill, I also considered that I would have to walk back up. My last Saturday shopping excursion had been fun, but climbing back up the hill with my bags of groceries was... challenging. And yes, I was out of shape, but you need to understand that "climbing back up the hill" is more like climbing a series of steep hills. My apartment was about six levels up from the beach. I had found sets of stairs as an alternative to hiking up the streets. These seemed easier (or maybe faster) than the steady walk up a street. They probably weren't, but I was good with whatever psychological games I needed to play to get me up the hill. Still, I cursed myself for not taking a taxi back.

I'll Take My Wins Where I Can Find Them

That Saturday was full of little victories.

I hit one more "big" grocery store, the Pingo Doce. I cannot find everything I want or need at one store so shopping is a matter of rotating through Aldi, Lidl, Continente, and now Pingo Doce, and then remembering where the hell you found avocado oil or the Biscoff cookies or full fat milk as opposed to two percent. I still hit my smaller neighborhood market to pick up necessities. Today those necessities were Oreos, Ruffles potato chips, and plain M&Ms. And cream and eggs and bread and meat and all that responsible stuff.

As I waited in line to get in, I realized that I was spending more on groceries than I normally would. I recognized that it was a symptom of insecurity. I normally don't have that much junk food in the house. Now I have it just in case I have a craving. Or if I start missing the States and my friends. I figure as I adapt, my food bill will go down. But right now, it's my only real expenditure and I am indulging myself.

One thing I have missed is prepped foods. While Costco rotisserie chicken is legendary and most American supermarkets carry rotisserie and fried chicken and other prepped meals, I haven't found that in Portugal. I think the Continente might have some. Saturday, I discovered some prepped meals at Pingo Doce. Since my "kitchen" had no real oven, I wished I had found this weeks ago. Still, I didn't order from the deli counter.

I watched to see how it worked—people went to a little machine and got a numbered ticket, just like the deli counters in the States. I listened to the exchanges, all in Portuguese. I don't want to be *that* American and assume someone will speak English. My Pimsleur Portuguese lessons had yet to include what to say at the grocery store and I was shy about approaching the counter. I realized—again—that my life will be a lot better here if I make the effort to learn the language.

I was slowly trying new foods. Near the deli counter I picked up a package of *croquette de picanha*. They looked like hush puppies or maybe donut holes. I asked myself, *How bad can they be?*

Spoiler Alert: They were neither hush puppies nor donut holes.

I was inspecting a pastry at the bakery counter when the baker pushed a package of six little pastries towards me, said a lot of stuff quickly in Portuguese that even if I had caught the words I would not have understood. I read the label: *pastéis de nata*. The famous Portuguese treat. I said to him in English, "You are a dangerous man." Neither of us knew it yet, but he was my new BFF.

On the way back, just a few doors down from the Pingo Doce, is TimTim's Chinese Restaurant. OMG! I hadn't had Chinese food in months. (How have I survived?) Their sign on the sidewalk said they were open for takeaway. I walked up the two flights of stairs (talk about being motivated!) and put in an order.

I waited in the sunshine, breathing in the fresh air. One or two people passed me on their way up from one street level to the next. The city is filled with these back stairways, short cuts from one street to another, one level to another. I was just now discovering that they are the rule, not the exception.

My order was ready and it was less expensive than I had calculated in my head—just under 15 euro. I tipped generously because restaurants and their staffers had taken a huge hit due to the pandemic. I told the woman, "You are saving my life," and she laughed. But she didn't know how nice it would be to have a meal that I didn't cook (my cooking is abysmal). She didn't know how much I have missed Chinese takeaway and pizza and Costco chicken. *Tonight*, I schemed in my head, *I will have a feast!* I was bubbling with happiness and anticipation.

It's All Scenic

I would say that I took the scenic route back, but honestly, it's all scenic. The two-mile trek back to my place involved many stops, some to rest and some to take pictures of the painted utility boxes. I am trying to be more "mindful" here, to take notice of the everyday things. I had seen the painted utility boxes on previous walks without really taking them in. On my return journey, I found them seemingly at every turn.

I walked along the beach road, just above Praia dos Pescadores. The beach was uncrowded, but busier than I had seen so far. I couldn't imagine how cold the water was—I have been spoiled by the warm waters of Hawaii, Mexico, the Caribbean, and Florida. I grew up in New England where stepping into the Atlantic usually sent a shockwave through your entire body. I was almost ready to dip my feet in here, even if it was cold. The waves weren't big, but the surfers were out, just happy to be in the water.

The climb home once again discouraged me. I was not conquering these hills. I was not magically getting in shape. (*I dunno, could be the Oreos and potato chips, Barb...*) It was discouraging. I felt old. Was I physically up for this new life? My next Airbnb was in town, much closer to all the stores and only halfway up a hill. It will be easier there, I told myself.

Let's Have Mikey Try It

I put the groceries away and looked up the word *picanha* on Google translate. I wanted to make sure it was not fish. Rump steak. Okay. I have never eaten a croquette anything in my life. I am not an adventurous eater but I am committed to trying a new food a week. I heated it in the microwave, wishing I had an oven because I knew that this was **NOT** the way to go with this thing. They are fried, so the microwave will screw up the texture. But even the microwave cannot ruin these things. They are GOOD! I had a new food. My discouragement vanished.

Next up was the *pastéis de nata*. I told myself it was my reward for not dying on the hills today. OMG! You have to come here just to eat these things! I am so glad I did not die before I ate one of these. A *pastel de nata* is a puff pastry shell with a sweet custard filling, carmelized on the top. I didn't know if you were supposed to use a knife and fork or if it was finger food. I ate it standing over the sink to catch the little flakes of puff pastry that didn't make it into my mouth. (*Sinful waste*, I thought to myself.) It is my new favorite thing and I was VERY GLAD there were six of them in the package. I was also glad that they were a two-mile walk from me because if they were close by, I was very certain I would gain 40 pounds in a week. I resisted the urge to binge on another— *"Pace yourself"*— but I planned on having one for dessert that night, after my Chinese food. These things are seriously yummy.

Must Do Better

I won't lie. I was more tired than I should have been. I had planned to walk the beach on Sunday but I was just not up for it. My exhaustion was part physical, of course. But it was also mental and emotional. Going grocery shopping induced a level of anxiety in me that was embarrassing so I tried to ignore it. I mean, it's grocery shopping. It's a simple activity. While only a limited amount of people were allowed in stores at a time, you were still inside, breathing through a mask, not sure if a COVID germ would somehow get through.

But it wasn't just COVID anxiety. Going out in public, to the store was like one of those scary movie montages where you are lost and weird laughing faces zoom in close to you. Very little on the shelves looked familiar. I saw splashes of color but didn't recognize brands or even what I was looking at. I tried to interpret the labels and my Internet connection on my phone didn't work because I didn't have the right SIM card. Things weren't where I expected them to be and if I found something once, there was no guarantee I would find it in the same spot the next time. When the clerk asked me a question, I had no idea what she was asking. She held up a plastic bag. Got it! I showed her my cloth bags. I paid by card because I still can't figure out the cash machines here and the currency exchanges were not open. I was super-self-conscious at the check-out, trying to bag up my groceries as fast as I could so I was not holding up the line. No one complained or stared; it was all me and my anxiety.

More than once, I wondered if moving here was a mistake. I couldn't go anywhere and explore places. I didn't know the language. I was in limbo as far as my immigration appointment. I didn't know anyone. I missed my friends. I missed my car. I missed how easy my life was back in the States: I knew where everything was and how everything worked. I was exhausted by a simple trip to the grocery store. Was I going to wash out of the expat life?

But I had tons of food in the house and work to do. Little by little I was learning about my new country, even if I couldn't explore beyond my first city. I reframed the inability to travel as something that took the pressure off me. For now, I didn't have to figure out car rentals or driving roundabouts or the train system. I loved that there was so little traffic in Albufeira but I didn't know if I was ready to head out on the A22. So, the lockdown was not as onerous for me as it was for most. It provided good cover for my cowardice. But soon I would have to step up to the plate. And I knew that I would. Really, there was no choice. In the meantime, I'd keep climbing the hills. And get that walk in on the beach.

Chapter Twelve

Airbnb Hopping

The first week of March approached and my two months were up at my first Airbnb. I still didn't have a working phone here, but I'd arranged for an Uber using my laptop. I had picked up very few things in the past two months, with the notable exception of the coffee maker which I packed back into its original box.

The day before I had walked over to the next Airbnb and picked up the key to my new place. I had been smart enough to overlap my accommodations by a day or two, so I could get into my new place, look around, and not have to be all in a crush to get all my things over in one trip.

The apartment was on the third floor, which was really the fourth floor. There was no elevator. My Uber driver let me off and helped me get my suitcases and bags to the stairs. My laptop bag was slung across my back. I started with the heaviest suitcase and lightest bag, taking them up two flights, then I went back down and retrieved the smaller suitcase and the bag with the coffee maker, then made a third trip down for the last two bags. I paused, huffing and puffing on the second floor. I repeated the process bringing everything up two more flights to my floor.

This Airbnb was bigger, with a dining table set at the front windows of the apartment, overlooking the street. There were two black leather and chrome couches, very low to the ground. The bedroom was a real bedroom with a closet and drawers and a view of the ocean. I settled my things in and hung some clothes in the closet. I love the packing cubes I use—I set up in these apartments the same way I set up in a hotel room: I take the whole packing cube, unzip the top and put it in the drawer. It also made packing to leave easier.

The bed had a very nice—and it turned out warm—duvet on it. I had had a king size bed for ten years. The slightly-smaller-than queen beds here take getting used to. I realized how spoiled I was in the everything-is-bigger US.

Best of all, the apartment had a lot of light, and felt much roomier. The leather couches weren't all that comfortable but more so than the loveseat in the last place.

The kitchen... well, it was an improvement, sort of. It was, again, a strip of sink, stove, and no counter space. The "kitchen" had a layer of grease that seemed like it had been there for a lifetime. A small, freestanding shelf unit separated the living room from the kitchen. It had pots and pans, a very old-fashioned toaster, and other random kitchen items on it. Did I mention there was no counter space? None. There were cabinets above the sink and stove holding a few glasses, various plates, and cups.

One cabinet for food. All the Airbnbs here seem to come with salt and pepper, olive oil, an odd assortment of tea bags, and whatever food was left from the last guest. I found a boxed pizza in the little freezer compartment of the under-the-counter refrigerator. Who knows how long it had been there? I tossed it.

I was afraid to light the gas oven, mostly because I thought it would leak gas and kill me in my sleep. The stove top had four small gas burners. Portuguese Airbnb owners apparently don't believe in deep sinks. This one was about four inches deep. As we say, if the entire front of your shirt isn't soaked, you obviously didn't do the dishes.

As I stood in the living area, looking at the kitchen, I realized that it was set up in a closet. This apartment was most likely a two bedroom, two bath that was split into two rental units. The living area had probably been a bedroom and the "kitchen" was the converted closet. I found it oddly interesting, but not particularly off-putting. People need to make money.

My first Airbnb had been in a strictly residential area. There was the one market down the hill and a few restaurants a short distance away. My new Airbnb was "in town" near the municipal building, just a short walk to the Pingo Doce and Continente grocery stores. And, I noted, relatively flat.

The area was filled with restaurants open for takeaway on a regular basis. I walked the neighborhood to get acquainted and took a picture of the menu board outside the closest restaurant. I could translate it when I got back to the apartment. All in all, I was happy to be closer to the center of Albufeira. Fewer hills, for starters, and within a few days, I felt relatively familiar with my new neighborhood.

Hoping for a Cancellation

I was rather anxiously scanning the Facebook expat groups. People were complaining that their SEF appointments were being canceled due to COVID. My appointment was set for the third week in April and I had discovered that I was totally unprepared for it. I needed a NIF (fiscal identification number) and a Portuguese bank account. My passport would expire in August and I needed to renew it before the appointment. I might have been the only immigrant hoping that my appointment would get postponed.

I managed to get my NIF done online. The gentleman who was doing it was very German and humorless. Those are two separate things. He's probably a downer at the biergarten, too. I had filled out the information online, uploaded a copy of my passport, and sent the money, somewhere in the range of $80 or $85. Now, I needed to take a picture of me "live" or allow him to take a picture of me live, an awkward process that required me to hold my laptop up to get a closeup of my face while pushing a button that was on the screen and really, you needed two people to do this. Most of the time I am happy to be single, but it's shit like this that makes me crazy. Maybe if I just had one more arm...

He was impatient. He didn't say it out loud, but I clearly heard "Stupid old woman" emanating from his brain. Snapping the picture took a couple of tries before we finally got it. He told me I would get my NIF in seven to ten days. Once I had the NIF, I could open a bank account. Once I opened the bank account, I could send my passport off to Lisbon to be renewed at the embassy. But I didn't know if I would have enough time to get this all done before my appointment in April. What if the passport was held up at the embassy?

I also needed to get passport pictures done for the SEF appointment. With everything in lockdown, that was going to be a little tricky. I needed to make copies of things, print things out, get my paperwork in order. I asked in one of the expat groups where I could get the pictures done and copies made. There was a place right by the supermarkets. Handy.

The NIF arrived via email. I downloaded and copied it, along with other paperwork, to a thumb drive. The copy place was great. They were open limited hours and there was a line outside, but they could print out the documents, make copies, *AND* do the passport photos. With the printout of my NIF (several copies made), I could go to a bank and set up an account.

Again, limited hours. And I had missed them.

I went back to the bank the next day, took a ticket and waited in a neatly spaced (two meters apart) line. The bank gentleman spoke fairly fluent English. He opened the account for me and showed me how to use the ATM so I could deposit the cash

I had brought to open the account. I was confused as to how it all worked: There's some sort of number you are assigned. Every time you log into your account online, you are asked for a variation of three of the seven numbers. That part I got. But I **think** he was showing me how I could go to certain ATMs without my card, use the number, and get cash out. Kind of cool.

He said my MultiBanco debit card would come in ten days. Did I want it sent to my address? That was a huge no. I had no access to the mailbox. For ten euros, they could have the card sent to the branch and I could pick it up there. That was a good deal to me.

I left with my bank account funded, an ATM card coming. I walked around the mall-like area where the bank is. I'd been to the Continente grocery that is just behind the bank. It is huge and has a flat escalator to the second floor so you can take your cart. Upstairs is mostly household goods and I found full-size hangers and clothespins to supplement the ten or so that were in the Airbnb. Little by little I was accumulating things I would need when I found my permanent place.

Which was another worry. I was halfway through my six months of accommodations necessary for my residency. Did I need to have six months from my April appointment? Or just six months from when I arrived in Portugal? One more thing I didn't know and needed to find out.

Then it got worse: I received an email from the Airbnb host where I was supposed to go in May. His guest couldn't travel and was stuck in Portugal. Could I find another place to stay?

Did I mention the anxiety involved in moving to a new country? I logged back onto Airbnb, looking for a place for May. I needed to find a permanent apartment as soon as possible, but in this case, the urgent gets done before the important.

I found a place to rent for a month in the nearby town of Ohlão. This actually worked out better for me—it was not nearly as far to go. I had wanted to check out northern Portugal and the canceled Airbnb was way up in Nazaré, north of Lisbon. Schlepping my worldly goods from one apartment in Albufeira to the next was hard enough. I pictured myself trying to pack everything up to get on a train to Lisbon, then whatever transport would be necessary to get to Nazaré, and then, most likely, I would need an Uber from there.

Portugal may be a small country with a pretty good public transportation system, but you do NOT want to move by public transit. And you don't want to spend six to eight hours carrying heavy bags. I don't, at least. I sent an email to the Nazaré Airbnb host that I was all set with another place, and my deposit was refunded almost immediately. No fuss, no muss.

My appointment with SEF was coming up in about a month and I felt like I was the ONLY immigrant in Portugal who hadn't had their appointment canceled. Really? If they had asked for volunteers, I would have been waving my arms frantically. Finally, the email came—my appointment was postponed until the end of September. Fantastic!

Because of all the cancellations and postponements, all of the temporary visas were extended to the end of the year. Between the new appointment and that, I felt like I could breathe a bit. I downloaded the passport application from the embassy website, went to the copy center to print it out, and had two color copies of my passport made. They did the passport pictures there, too.

I filled out the form, then went to CTT, the post office, to mail my passport to the Embassy in Lisbon. Before I did that, I had the clerk notarize one of the color copies of my passport. We're supposed to carry our passports on us at all times, or at least that was my vague understanding. I felt vulnerable mailing my passport off, worried that it wouldn't come back at all, much less in the three-week average turnaround time. I paid to have the passport returned via DHL. Another extra expense because I have no mailbox. But I now had a longer time frame to get the new passport and find an apartment. I breathed a little easier.

Chapter Thirteen

Encountering Expat Weirdness

The days were getting warmer, but it was still cold to this Florida girl. I'd started working from bed in the mornings, basking in the warmth of the duvet. It felt indulgent. The truth was that the space heater in this Airbnb was a huge gas-fueled thing that scared me. Neither Airbnb had smoke alarms or carbon monoxide detectors in them. I didn't know if it was a lack on the Airbnb owners' part, or if they just weren't required here. I couldn't get the heater to work properly and, as with the oven, I had no desire to die by carbon monoxide poisoning. Or whatever the gas was.

The view from my bedroom window almost makes up for the kitchen.

By mid-morning, it would be warm enough for me to venture out of bed, get showered, and move myself out to the living area. If you're thinking that my new life was fairly solitary at this point, you're not wrong. Between COVID lockdowns, not knowing the language, and being introverted, my odds of making friends were pretty low.

But, I was now in several online expat groups and one was having a meetup at an outdoor restaurant. One of the women reached out and invited me and I was more than ready to get out of the house and eat a decent meal. Restrictions were loosening up and more cafés and restaurants were opening their terraces for actual sit-down eating.

We met at a designated spot and walked up to the restaurant. No one was there. She had gotten the time wrong, so we had a cup of coffee before walking back down to the main street.

A bit anticlimactic, but I was okay with it. We met for coffee several times over the next few weeks. She is British, worked in the States for a number of years. She made it into Portugal just before Brexit, but residency was going to be a financial stretch for her.

She is older than I am and seemed to know her way around. I was surprised when I found out she had only been in Portugal for a few months more than I had. I am once again reminded that I have to be less passive about things, to take more control of my life. Really, to stop assuming that everyone knows more than I do about all things Portugal. There's a lot of misinformation in the expat groups and, as in most aspects of life, more people are feeling their way through than you would suspect. The phrase "Consider the source" floated up to the top of my consciousness. It would come in handy.

We had some things in common and while she was not going to be my new best friend, it was nice to have someone to meet for coffee and have a chat.

She was dating, meeting men via Tinder, which is a thing here. Maybe it's a thing everywhere. I am *so* not-tuned-in to online dating that it took me a bit to realize I was confusing Tinder with Grindr in my head. But I was kind of surprised that meeting people via online apps is now the way it's done. Maybe it was due to the pandemic—people can't go places and randomly meet people. And, if you think about it, that's probably not the most efficient way to find your soul mate, hoping you'll bump into The One in some sort of meet-cute, rom-com scenario. I mean, hey, I've always depended on that and so far, it's worked for me, but then again, I'm still single. Whatever.

She took me to her "phone guy" and got me set up with a phone. She unsubtly reminded him that she was bringing him business, angling for some free service or other. I was embarrassed that she was so obvious, but she wasn't and that's okay. End result is that I now had a phone that worked in Europe. I had no one to call (with the exception of this one new acquaintance), but maybe it would solve my Uber problem.

So, sum total of our relationship: several coffee meetings and one lunch. I tell you this because of what came next.

We were at her apartment, having coffee and some sort of nosh from the neighborhood bakery. She mentioned that she needed to dye her hair. Then she asked me if I would do it for her.

I stopped chewing.

Seriously?

Is it just me or is that kind of weird?

Or is this what friends do? Dye their hair together? Is it an expat thing?

I was in panic mode because I have no idea what's involved in dying hair. I was sick for a large part of seventh grade, which seems to have been the exact time they taught Girl 101. I have pretty much had the same hair style since high school. I basically suck at all things girl. I remembered a friend saying she and her sisters all got together and dyed their hair, but they had known each other all their lives.

Like... it's kind of intimate and a weird "ask," yeah?

I swallowed.

"Um, I don't know anything about dying hair."

"You don't dye your hair?"

"I barely brush it."

I was pretty sure she didn't believe me. I have very little grey in my hair for someone my age, but then, I didn't have kids. Or a husband. Life's been good to my hair color.

"Well, it's fairly easy to do."

At 63 years old, one of the greatest achievements in my life is I have learned how to say no. And this one was a dead stop.

"You definitely do NOT want me dying your hair. I cannot do that."

We finished our coffees, speaking awkwardly about other things, and I toddled on home, weirded out and wondering if I was over-reacting. Over the next few days, I asked a few of my gal pals in the States if it was a weird request. I was looking for validation and I got it. But maybe it was a cultural thing?

I had made another coffee friend in the meantime, another British woman, younger than I am. She had recently left a very good job with a lovely severance package. She was doing some consulting and knew that she would need to find a real job again, when the world returned to normal. I have more in common with her than most of the expat retirees, whose lives seem to revolve around golf and social occasions, however limited.

We met for coffee and, since she had a car, we were able to explore a bit, too. We'd been to neighboring towns to poke around, have lunch or a coffee. Really, it was a chance to chat and get out of the house.

I asked her if I missed something in the expat rules about dying each other's hair. She started laughing. No, that was a weird request.

I finally felt vindicated.

I'm never quite sure what's normal. I have been living my own little life in my own bubble for decades. I haven't worked a corporate job in 20 years. Most of my socializing is with other entrepreneurs at networking meetings and seminars. I know that I am... shall we say a bit stilted socially? I mean, sure, you can take me to a cocktail party and I can pretend to be interested in small talk, but inside I am screaming and I suspect most of the other guests are, too. The problem is that I will be the one to mention it at some point in the evening. Out loud. So, when I get a request I consider odd, I always have to ask myself if "normal" people do this.

Turns out, I am fairly normal and frighteningly average, with a special talent for attracting batshit crazy people.

Yay?

Well, maybe not batshit crazy. But I do seem to attract non-stop talkers. Who always have some sort of drama going on. Do you know what I mean? They are the people who call you up and talk for 45 minutes to an hour about themselves. They only ask how you're doing when you say you have to go. The question is meant to keep you on the line longer so you can hear more about them.

It's my fault—I am GREAT at pretending to listen to people. And while I'm pretending, I am usually reminding myself that the person is lonely or needs to vent or whatever.

I have vowed that in my new life in Portugal, I will not be adding any more of these people. I am a senior citizen: I am edging closer and closer to death and I still have a lot of stuff I need to do! I do NOT have the time for any more people like this. Dance card is full.

No Matter Where You Go...

The days were slipping by and I had settled into a bit of a routine. I worked with my clients. I got groceries. I met with the two people I knew in Portugal for coffee from time to time. I was figuring things out, little by little, but there were no big changes, no epiphanies, no feeling like "OMG! I'm living in Europe. I'm European!"

I was, as I both suspected and feared, just me, living in a different country. I told myself it was because we couldn't travel and most things were still shut down. But the truth was obvious.

It may be a bit telling that one of my favorite movies is a weird cult film from the '80s: *The Adventures of Buckaroo Banzai Across the 8th Dimension*. Peter Weller with hair. Yum. Actually, it seems like everyone was in that movie: Christopher Lloyd, John Lithgow, Rosalind Cash, Ellen Barkin, Jeff Goldblum (and the stars just keep on coming). Jamie Lee Curtis was in the original opening scene that was scrapped.

To get us back on track here, in a movie teeming with classic one-liners, Weller gets to say, "No matter where you go, there you are."

I am me, just in a new country. I'm an introvert. I have trouble making conversation with strangers. I *hate* to ask for help, not out of pride but out of awkwardness. Now I am in a situation where I need to ask directions, ask for help, meet new people. I can do it. I have done it before. In part, it's more a matter of getting back to who I used to be than becoming a different person. But I also know that I am hiding behind..., well, two things: the COVID lockdowns and the fact that I am not yet in my permanent place. I have another month in Albufeira and I don't see the sense in creating relationships in a place where I am not staying.

And right then, not making a lot of new friends was the path of least resistance.

I recognized it and granted myself some grace. I was not quite four months into this experience, during a very weird time in human history, and I was old enough to know that change takes time. Even changing back.

Chapter Fourteen

The Great Portuguese Apartment Hunt

Finding a Long-Term Rental Is NOT Easy.

May arrived, and with it a loosening up of lockdown, and a new Airbnb. I had moved to a town I couldn't pronounce. My British friend Jo and I played with it, bouncing the nasal pronunciation of the ão of Ohlão back and forth between us. Two syllables or three? Accent on the first or last? Either way, I was in my new place.

This Airbnb was the best apartment yet. It was a REAL apartment: a fully outfitted eat-in kitchen (very clean), a separate bedroom, nice sized bath. The living room was a bit of an odd space, but the entire apartment had lots of light, was clean, and well outfitted. I now understood what a "super-host" is.

Getting to the apartment was a bit rocky. It is located in the historic center of Olhão, a rabbit warren of cobblestone back streets and pedestrian-only walkways. Which meant my Uber driver couldn't bring me to the actual address. (Something to consider when booking a place to stay.) We had to park a few streets away and try to find the address—no easy feat. I finally stopped and asked in a shop and the shopkeeper, who had obviously done this before, stepped out of the shop, and pointed me back to the cross "street" just steps away.

I rang the bell and the host was there to greet me and help out. We dropped the bags and I went back with the driver to get the rest of my things. The owner left and I settled in to my new digs.

The windows were open and there was a warm breeze coming in. The apartment was on a corner and there were lots of people walking by, talking and laughing. It was a busy area and after the isolation of lockdowns, I started to feel like I was finally in Portugal.

When I first arrived in Albufeira, I was more than a tad enchanted by the cobblestone sidewalks or calçadas. Until I tried to walk on them in the rain. They're slicker than goose shit. Even in dry weather, walking on cobbles takes a little getting used to. Portuguese women navigate them at a rapid clip in spike heels without blinking, of course. I find these women astonishing, awe-inspiring, and intimidating. I am proud to say that I can now navigate the cobbles at a matching clip, in my Fila running shoes. If it hasn't rained.

One of the "benefits" of cobblestones is that they create a distinctive sound. They also *amplify* sound. *REALLY* well. You can hear a car (or a horse-drawn carriage) approaching on a cobblestone street from at least a block away. That's especially handy in areas where there are a lot of pedestrians. The buildings in this particular area are about 12 feet apart which creates narrow "canyons" where people walk. The result is that sound is amplified and carried for at least a block. I could distinctly hear the conversations of people walking in the area long before I could see them. I could hear the trash containers being emptied several blocks away. A bicycle crash around the corner was as loud as a car crash. (No fatalities or injuries, but both bicyclists chose to stay in place for about 20 minutes while they gathered their wits.)

One of the pedestrian streets in Olhão.

Not too far away is the Nossa Senhora do Rosário Church, built between 1681 and 1698. The bell tolls the hours and half hours and puts a fine bit of punctuation to the expression, "clear as a bell." Although it was several blocks away, the first time I heard it ring out, I thought I was standing in the bell tower. For reals. Because...cobblestones. Everything is amplified and echoes. (Think of the cartoon cat who gets hit hard and his head turns into a bell ding-donging loudly. *THAT* loud.) It took me about a week to stop jumping every time they rang out. I also learned to expect the second round of church bell chimes that came two minutes later, in case you missed any noise the first time. (For my Boston friends, think of Dave Maynard, suffering through *Community Auditions*: "And in reprise...")

During the month I was there, I got used to the volume of the bells but I never figured out the pattern of the chimes. Sometimes there would be a series of nine chimes at odd hours, an extensive peal of bells usually at 5:30 pm or sometimes at 4:30, followed by 33 chimes representing Christ's years on Earth, maybe? One day, the bells tolled 78 times. (I counted.) I'm assuming it was for a funeral and that was the age of the deceased. A good long life marked. But I was really just making it up in my head—trying to assign a reason. I mentally shrugged—it could be true.

Olhão is a working city with a strong Moorish appearance. It started as a fishing village and, during the sieges of Cadiz and Gibralter, the town's enterprising boatmen made their fortunes supplying services to both sides of the conflict. While Olhão has easy access to some of the most beautiful beaches in the Algarve, it is mainly a working town, off the beaten track for most tourists, but starting to gain popularity as other tourist towns become more expensive.

All this is a way of saying it was very noisy in this area. But I grew used to it, the same as you would grow used to the hum of traffic if you lived in a city or the shouts of children if you lived near a school. This section of town is filled with small shops and mom-and-pop cafés. (Yes, of course I quickly found a favorite.) From early in the morning to about midnight, there was always someone walking by. I listened in on conversations from two stories up, trying to recognize a word or two of Portuguese from my limited vocabulary. Mostly I enjoyed hearing the voices raised in greeting and the background chatter of everyday life.

I liked Olhão. It is flat, for starters! It had things that I have missed: a Chinese restaurant *and* a Mexican restaurant. I was close to all the shops. It was a five-minute walk to the waterfront. I could walk to the train station and a little beyond that is the Algarve Shopping Center, a real shopping center. The hours and number of people allowed in at any one time were still limited, but the entire town has more conveniences and more going on. Not that Albufeira isn't a happening place. But Albufeira is definitely a tourist town and with travel restrictions and lockdowns, it was pretty subdued. I hit Olhão just as things were truly opening up.

This Airbnb was a one-month rental and I had resolved to find a permanent apartment rather than move into another

Airbnb. I needed a six-month lease for my SEF appointment, and the sooner I had it in hand, the more prepared I would feel.

I spent time on the Portuguese equivalent of Craigslist (olx.pt) and Idealista, a real estate site. I quickly figured out that many of the "long-term" rentals in the Algarve are not so long-term: They rent out from October or November until May. Then you need to clear out so the landlord can rent it by the week to tourists in the summer. That was not going to work for me.

I found an apartment that was in my budget and what I was looking for. My friend Jo picked me up and we drove over to Tavira. We spent several hours walking around, visiting the ruins of the castle, having coffee, and we both loved the vibe of the town. We met up with the landlord to check the apartment. It was perfect: just refinished, modern, a two bedroom, two bath, with a parking space in the garage below. The rent was in the right range. It had central heat and air. It was clean. And... I didn't like it.

Jo understood immediately. We were already in love with the Tavira vibe, traditional style houses with gorgeous tile work and vines of flowers working their way up buildings to balconies. This was a perfectly modern apartment in a nondescript apartment block, on a street close to a school. It was perfect for a young family with kids that would go to that school. It was not perfect for me.

We thanked the owner and walked back across the river to sit in the sun and have lunch. We agreed that this is the town

I wanted to live in. When I got back to my apartment, I narrowed my search to apartments in the Tavira area. The listings mentioned the neighborhoods of Tavira, but I had no concept of the geography. I would flip back and forth between listings and a map of the area, trying to figure out how far from town an apartment was.

There's no MLS here. Real estate agents show you only the listings that their office has. If you want to see another property that is listed by a different company, you contact them. People will work with several agents to find a place to buy or rent.

A week later, we went back. I had an appointment with a real estate agent to show me an apartment in the village of Santa Luzia, about four kilometers from Tavira. She said the apartment was next to a bakery. Already it sounded good.

We met the agent and she brought us up to meet with the landlord. They spoke Portuguese together. (The agent speaks five or six languages. Not too intimidating!) The landlord's English was halting, but he was friendly. His handyman was still fixing up the place. The place needed paint and cleaning, but it was perfect. Just about everything about it was perfect.

It is on the main street of the village, which parallels the Tavira Channel. It faces the south so it has wonderful sun exposure; tons of light. From the front balcony I can look out over the water and the barrier island, and see the Atlantic. The fishing boats dock right across the street, bringing in their catch to the fish clearing house. I wondered if the town was going to smell fishy, but it was low tide and I didn't catch a whiff.

There is a restaurant below the apartment, the bakery is next door at street level. The floors are tile. The ceilings are high, nine feet at least. The kitchen is good-sized. There are two bedrooms but only one bath. I live alone and only occasionally have guests; I can deal. There's a little inner courtyard in the L created between the second bedroom and the kitchen.

But it was a little bit out of my budget. By about €100 per month. I told the agent I would let her know and Jo and I went into Tavira for coffee and my next appointment.

The next apartment was in the central district of Tavira. Narrow, cobblestone streets, traditional style building. We climbed the stairs to the main floor of the apartment. This apartment got some sunlight, but nothing compared to the apartment we had just looked at. In the apartment directly across the street, two dogs were guarding their territory—loudly. They started barking when we went into the building and five minutes later, hadn't stopped. The apartment was a townhouse. The first floor had the kitchen, living room, dining room, and bath. The bedrooms were upstairs. There was a spiral staircase. Very cool. I always wanted a spiral staircase!

We went upstairs and looked at the two bedrooms. Smallish compared to the last place. And the deal killer: no bathroom upstairs. I would have to go *up* that staircase after two or three glasses of wine. I would have to traipse *down* the spiral staircase in the middle of the night to pee. Suddenly, the spiral staircase I always wanted hit reality: I am 63 years old and the staircase will most likely kill me at some point. Between the dogs and the staircase, this one was a no.

The agent had one more apartment across the river. We followed her over to see the neighborhood, but we couldn't get into the building. Couldn't even look in the windows. The neighborhood was a bit depressing and like the first apartment I looked at, the building was just a personality-less pile of cement blocks.

We had a lovely lunch and wandered around the shops, talking about the apartments we'd seen. Hands-down, the Santa Luzia apartment was the winner. When I got home that night, I called the agent and told her I'd like to take it, but the price was a bit out of my range. If the landlord could come down €50 a month, I'd take it as-is and he wouldn't need to have it painted.

The agent was excellent. She made the deal and provided the lease, along with a version in English. It asked for one month's deposit and the first month's rent. I was suspicious. I had read horror stories in the expat groups about hidden terms, and bad landlords, and all sorts of things that can go wrong. It is standard for the landlord to ask for first, last, and *two* months' deposit. Some landlords wanted six months' rent in advance! I spent time on Google translate, making sure that there was nothing in the Portuguese lease that wasn't in the English lease. They were a match.

I signed the lease and she brought it to the landlord to sign. I was set to move in on June 1st, about two weeks away. I asked if he wanted the money sent over. No, I could pay him when

I got there. In cash. My Spidey sense was prickling, but I remembered as a landlord I wanted my deposits and first month's rent in cash. My Airbnb was good until June 5th; if anything went wrong, I could extend or find another Airbnb. I spent the next ten days mostly being impatient. But the impatience was superficial.

I realized that I was, perhaps for the first time in months, relaxed. Things were falling into place. I had my new passport. I had my NIF and my bank account. And now, I finally had a real place to live. The impatience was really excitement.

The following Tuesday I took the train into Tavira to make arrangements for Internet at my new, somewhat permanent digs. Internet providers in Portugal have about the same reputation as Internet providers in the US. That may be a saga for another time.

When I say in a casual way, "I took the train to Tavira" please know that there was nothing casual about it because it was another new learning experience for me. I went to the train station the day before just to suss it out. The charming young man at the window told me that I needed to buy my ticket the day of, how much it would cost (less than €5 roundtrip—such a deal!), and what times the trains ran. The next morning, I walked in like a boss, bought my ticket, and sat outside to wait ten minutes for the train which was pretty much on time. The conductor came by with a cheery *Bom Dia!* and punched my ticket. I was ridiculously happy. Not even going to pretend to be cool about it. My first REAL TRAIN RIDE! I mean, unless the T counts.

I decided to walk from the Tavira train station to the Gran Plaza (less than three kilometers) where I could find all three Internet providers in one location. The walk turned out to be longer than it had to be because I was using Waze, which is designed for cars. I went up (of course) and over, instead of just down and across. Yes, I had managed to find the hills in Tavira. Because I wasn't on a tight schedule, the extra walking didn't cause stress or tension. It may have caused a slight blister.

I went back and forth between the three providers, had a coffee and donut, thought over my options, and went with one that I was pretty sure was a (small) mistake but would do for now. *If it is a mistake*, I thought, *I will fix it*. I was relaxed about it. I managed to find my way out of the Gran Plaza (I'm sure there's an easier entrance and exit which I vowed to find next time) and since I now recognized the area I was in, decided to walk into the centro district of town and reward myself with lunch. I'd hate to burn off more calories than I had taken in with a mere coffee and donut. Have to keep my weight up...

A restaurant chose me. Well, the lovely young lady at the hostess stand greeted me as I stopped to read the board listing the pratos do dia (plates of the day). Several choices appealed and she offered a menu in English. Most of the restaurants have menus that include several languages: Portuguese, English, German, French, Spanish. Algarve restaurants have the United Nations of menus.

I ordered the piri-piri chicken, always good and for me, always a safe bet. I opted for the boneless version, sat back with my still water, and looked out over the Gilão River, watching people and the occasional car go by. There was a group of Spanish women, sets of mothers and daughters enjoying a lunch filled with much laughter and over-talking, the way people do when they know each other so well.

It's all about presentation. The Gilão River is in the background.

An English couple was seated at the next table. I was hearing more and more English spoken which meant that Portugal was opening up to tourism to some extent. I was hesitant to speak to them—do you speak to someone else who speaks your language in a foreign country *just because* they speak your language? Is it needy? Is it impolite to initiate conversation? Is it impolite not to? I was back at the seventh-grade dance, not knowing how things worked. I minded my own business, enjoying my meal and the day, watching patrons come and go, listening to the maitre d' greet people as they passed by, inviting them to dine.

I finished my meal, ordered a coffee, and sat back. It was warm, but not too warm. I felt like I was finally living the European lifestyle I had imagined for myself. The English woman excused herself and less than a minute later, the man, a corporate type even in casual clothes, spoke to me.

He said, "You look completely comfortable sitting there."

I said, "I feel like a cat, lazy and content."

We chatted. The woman returned. They were visiting—not their first trip and not their last. He asked the question that continues to stump me: *Why did I choose Portugal?* It sounds flaky to say I just did. But basically, I just did. It ticked off all my boxes. We passed a pleasant ten minutes and then they went on their way. I caught a taxi back to the train station (I am getting wiser), and rode the train back to my Airbnb.

I thought about the man's opening comment. I am much more relaxed here. My time is my own, for the most part. I work, yes, but because of the time zone difference, I have a lot more leeway in scheduling. I don't feel the pressure of having to hustle and grind and always be competing.

There are stressors, of course. Not speaking the language is one. Trying to learn the language is another. I decided to take the pressure off myself on that by allowing that it might take more than listening to the Michel Thomas lessons *once* to become fluent.

It is merely inconvenience when I can't quite figure out what I am looking at in the grocery store, even with the Google translate app. I may have made a mistake in the Internet service I chose. If I did, it would be about a €100 mistake. It was not going to wipe me out and easily fixable. If I got on the train going the wrong way, I would have stopped at the next station and changed direction. (I didn't. I'm very proud.)

For some reason, everything seems fixable here. I have slowed my roll and I am getting more things done. There's a lesson in there.

My friend Jay often says about someone he admires, "He is on-center." It's his way of summing up that someone knows who they are and is comfortable with it. They are confident and relaxed.

Portugal has given me space. It has given me room to breathe—room that I didn't know I needed—just by its pace and scale. Slowly, week by week, I am relaxing into being who I am.

Chapter Fifteen

Creating a New Comfort Zone in Portugal

Finally! A place where I can truly unpack all my stuff!

Ever the trooper, Jo helped me move my belongings, which fortunately, still weren't much. In my five months here, I haven't bought many things mostly because I haven't needed them, and partly because I knew I would have to move them several times. (And really, most of the stores were closed!)

The Airbnbs came furnished including, of course, sheets and towels. The kitchens were "fully" equipped. I had bought a few things along the way: some kitchen utensils and dish towels, some office supplies, toiletries, and cleaning supplies. I could still put all my possessions in my two suitcases, laptop bag, and now, several tote bags. The coffee maker packed into its original box. And was transported with the reverence it deserved.

My new apartment came furnished, as many do. The dining table has six straight back chairs and there is a low (all the couches here are low, I swear!) L-shaped sofa. No other chairs, but that's okay. It's only me. The bedrooms are each outfitted with a double bed and twin night stands, each with small lamps, including two of the ugliest lamps I have ever seen, none suitable for reading.

The closets here—why aren't US closets like this? The closets have hanging space and a built-in chest of drawers, plus low shelves, and a higher shelf that runs the full length. They have sliding doors, one of which is a full-length mirror. My bedroom, which faces the front and therefore has a view of the channel, also has another set of built-in drawers next to the closet and three deep shelves above it. So efficient. For the first time that I can remember, I have more drawer and closet space than clothes and books and papers. It's an odd feeling, but I like it. The empty bookshelves make me a little sad, though. I miss my books.

Even though the landlord had cleaners come through, I wiped down the shelves and drawers before putting my things away.

My landlord provided two new mattress pads for the beds and pointed out that he added a new toilet seat. I laughed and told him how much I appreciated that. When I had rental property, I always put new toilet seats in for new tenants. It's not a law in the States, but it should be. I don't know if it's a law here or if he was just being nice. More than likely, it needed changing out. I didn't care; I appreciated it.

One of the best things my mother taught me was to make up the bed first thing when you move. She said, "You're going to be exhausted after moving, unpacking, and cleaning all day, and want to fall into bed. You will not have the energy to make it if you wait until you're going to bed." I've followed that advice in every move and she has never been wrong. I always appreciate having the bed made at the end of moving day.

I put the new mattress pad on my bed and then made it up with my new sheets. Both beds had bedspreads which I would eventually change out, but they would certainly do for now. After staying in Airbnbs, I wasn't nearly as weirded out about sleeping on someone else's pillows as I might have once been.

The Kitchen

The kitchen looked clean at first glance, but then I looked a little more closely. Or felt. As happens, there was a thin layer of grease in the stove area and I could tell that while everything had been wiped down, it hadn't really been deep-cleaned. I am not a good housekeeper but I like to at least start with things clean. After that, it's my own dirt and I'm okay with that.

The kitchen came "fully equipped" in its own quirky way. The cabinets and shelves were stuffed with dishes, glasses, various kitchen gadgets. There was silverware in the drawer but a strange assortment: Five forks, eight butter knives of varying straightness, three regular size teaspoons, seven large tablespoons, a plethora of the little demitasse spoons that you get with your coffee everywhere. A few pieces matched; most didn't. It looked like previous tenants had accumulated this mish-mosh of silverware by stealing from local restaurants. I thought of my relatively-new set back in storage. And sighed.

I spent three days cleaning and then sorting through all the various dishes, pots and pans, gadgets. I ended up with two "sets" of dishes: one plain white from a couple of different sources and another a swirl pattern in blues and greens. I counted 14 wine glasses, two beer glasses, a shot glass, and a cognac balloon glass. No drinking glasses. Two coffee mugs. Three cups, one saucer. I found three French presses and a stovetop espresso maker. I had to admire the priorities on display here.

I sorted through everything, found a set of pots and lids that seemed to match up and two (out of four or so) frying pans that weren't too warped. I stored all the stuff I would not be using in the cabinet over the fridge which I can't easily reach anyway. The rest went into a box labeled "Landlord."

And the Accumulation of Stuff Begins Again

I made at least half a dozen trips back and forth to the local mall in the first few weeks, getting a second set of sheets, a duvet cover, odds and ends that I needed around the house. I also realized that the "dongle" device I got for Wi-Fi was not going to cut it and signed up with an Internet/TV service.

I got to know the local Uber drivers. They always started off speaking to me in Portuguese—it turns out Barbara is a common name in Portugal and they assumed I was Portuguese. That lasted about ten seconds—until there was that awkward silence after the exchange of *bom dias* and I would ask in a small voice, "*Fala inglês?*"

One of my favorite drivers filled me in on local history, the fishing industry, his grown children, and the goings on around town. Another seemed to be a local celebrity. As we came down the main street in the village, people would wave at him or shout a greeting.

"Do you know everybody in Santa Luzia?" I asked.

He laughed. "I used to own a restaurant here, but it closed during COVID." He and his wife were rehabbing a guesthouse in the interior of the country. Driving for Uber was helping pay the bills while most everything was shut down. Another time, we were overtaken by a car that honked at him. He laughed and waved. "That's my wife," he explained. "She's driving today, too."

A third driver would take me on my many trips to the Pingo Doce grocery store. He'd have a coffee while I shopped, work on his books, and then drive me back. That saved me from having to wait anywhere from ten minutes to half an hour for a new driver to show up.

Restaurants were open with outside seating and the bakery next door was the local gathering place. I could sit on my balcony and watch all the comings and goings. I started to recognize various locals but with my lack of language skills, my interactions did not go much beyond a cheerful *bom dia!* and a smile.

The Uber drivers and the staff at the bakery were the only people I knew and really, the only people who knew me. I was in the village but still very much outside of it. It was time to start making my new life.

Exploring the Local Beaches

My apartment is on the "frontline" of town, meaning the waterfront, and when I moved in, I knew that July and August would be busy months. Santa Luzia has access to two of the prettiest beaches along the Ria Formosa (or at least we like to think so, but really, they are!). Fortunately, the village is recommended as a "day trip" for tourists, not a place to spend a week or two. For the most part, the tourists come, visit the beaches, have lunch or dinner at one of the restaurants, and leave again, heading for their hotels or Airbnbs in nearby towns. I have spotted a few Airbnbs here, but no hotels. We are not a late-night town.

Towards the end of June, beginning of July, the uptick in tourists was noticeable. One night, young people were singing and partying almost into the wee hours of the morning. I don't know if the GNR came by or it was just closing time, but the noise stopped about 12:30. Normally cars don't honk and people stop making noise by 11:00 pm. Our biggest traffic jam is when five or six cars have to wait for 20 seconds while passengers get into or out of cars near the bakery. People honked impatiently this week. They were not the norm. *They are not our people*, I thought to myself. I may have even sniffed.

It is said that life is a series of trade-offs and I understand that very well. Prior to the pandemic, I was already, shall we say, a tad overweight. Then I gained the dreaded "COVID 19"—those extra pounds that packed on after months of staying indoors and testing sour dough bread recipes. My clothes were uncomfortably tight. Fortunately, we were all living in sweatpants for a year.

But now that we were out and about, albeit cautiously, it was time to shed a few of those pounds or at least stop gaining. So, of course I chose an apartment next door to the best bakery in town. With fantastic croissants. Which is where the trade-off comes in.

Fortunately, my new digs are also well-placed for taking a daily walk. I can walk out my front door, turn left, and follow the sidewalk all the way into Tavira. Or I can turn right and follow the sidewalk all the way to Praia do Barril. Most days I turn right. It's almost exactly 5,000 steps to the entrance of the beach and back to my place.

I earn that croissant, damn it!

One day, as I stood at the entrance of Praia do Barril I thought, *it's time to check out that beach*. Praia do Barril is one of three beaches on the Ilha de Tavira, part of the Ria Formosa National Park. To get there, you cross a bridge and follow a boardwalk out and over the dunes. There's a series of signs with information on the ecology of the area—sea life, birds, flora. They are also handy if you need to stop and catch your breath, but don't want anyone to know that you are DYING.

It's a Hike

Little did I know that the walk from the entrance to the actual beach would add another four or five thousand steps to my walk—almost doubling it. There is a little train that runs people back and forth from the entrance to the beach (about €3 round trip), but I was there early in the day and it hadn't started running yet. Optimist that I am, I would have opted to walk anyway. For the record, optimism isn't always well-placed.

Be prepared: It's a bit of a hike (1.3 km each way).

But well worth it.

The beach itself is a gorgeous stretch of soft, white sand that even in the summer tourist season provides enough space to relax and if you walk a bit, have some privacy. Praia do Barril is a blue flag beach, a designation that is awarded yearly by the Foundation for Environmental Education. Blue flag beaches must meet international standards for environmental management, facilities, water quality, and safety. I'm pretty sure Barril exceeds those standards.

I had previously taken the ferry over to Terra Estreita—the beach at the other end of the island. The sand was hot-hot-hot and going ankle deep in the water froze my leg to the thigh. I remembered the water in Maine being this cold. As a kid, I would take a running plunge into it—best to do it all at once. As an adult, and having spent 30-plus years in the warm waters of Hawaii, Baja, the Caribbean, and Florida, I made the executive decision to not go in. Probably ever. But this beach has its charms; it's a little funky, not fancy. There's a snack bar and chair rentals, lifeguards, and bathroom facilities. The basics. While locals hit both beaches, Terra Estreita seems to be more local than Barril.

Praia do Barril has more options and facilities than Terra Estreita. There are full-service restaurants, for starters. Museu do Atum is actually a restaurant and mini-museum combined. There's also the Barril Beach Café and Blue Beach Bar. You can rent a sunbed with an umbrella for the day or bring your own chair, mat, or towel. There are restrooms and showers. In the summer, there are lifeguards on duty. You can also rent kayaks, paddleboards, and go sailing. In short, a full-service beach.

Tuna Industry

I was at the beach early, before things really opened up, which made it very private and quiet. I took the opportunity to poke around a bit. From about 1840 to 1967, Praia do Barril's economy revolved around blue fin tuna and it was home to about 80 tuna fishermen and their families during season. The buildings on the beach today are the original "fishermen's huts" but don't let the word "hut" fool you. These are permanent structures. This was a thriving community from April through October, with living facilities, warehouses, offices, a canteen, and a school house. The blue fin tuna moved to other waters about mid-20th century and the tuna industry gradually died out.

Which brings us to...

Cemiterio das Ancoras

On one section of the dunes is the Cemetery of Anchors, over 100 anchors placed in rows. Anchors were actually used as gear in the tuna fishing industry. They were part of a complex fishing system along with floats and nets. The anchors were lowered into the sea or placed along the beaches and were used to keep the nets in place. It took 8 to 12 men to lift the smaller anchors and up to 20 men for the larger anchors. When the blue fin tuna's migratory pattern changed, the anchors were left behind.

Cemiterio das Ancoras at Praia Barril.

The area's economy turned to tourism and Praia do Barril has transformed the fishermen's huts into the facilities that make this one of the top beaches in the Algarve.

PSA: Don't Be Surprised

If you walk a couple of kilometers to the west on Barril, you will find the official nude beach: Praia do Homem Nu. What can I say? Use strong sunblock. Actually, I didn't go that far, though I'm pretty sure the beach would have been empty at that time of day. But, it's there if you want it. I'm afraid my nude beach days are behind me.

It's Not all Castles and Pastéis de Nata

One of the hardest pieces of my day—still—is resisting the urge to run downstairs to the bakery and get something delicious. The bakery is no help at all in my fight to lose the extra pounds.

It sits there, like a spider in a web, just waiting for me to wander in...

Ah, the dangers of Portugal! Too many good pastries available on every corner. Articles on the expat life focus on all the benefits, all the good things and fun stuff and you might think, reading glossy magazines on international life, that we spend our days eating in quaint, out-of-the-way and incredibly inexpensive restaurants, drinking bottles of amazingly good wine from family wineries, and exploring castles. (Well, I *was* hanging out at a castle last weekend...)

But there are frustrations and setbacks that come with the life—things you need to adjust to and very little immediate gratification. My test run with Amazon Spain let me know that I will not be able to order something and have it show up at my door the next day.

More than once, I have done a lot more walking than I wanted to. One weekend, I took the train to meet up with Jo in Loule. The Uber driver was from Lisbon and dropped me at the wrong train station. I wasn't yet familiar enough with Tavira to figure out that was what happened. (Oh, the things I learn the hard way!) I also didn't know I could hop on the train there and pay the conductor as he came through, so I started hiking back, heading in the general direction of the main train station. This involved some hills, of course. And lots of steps. Lots.

I was hot, sweaty, tired, and about ready to give up when I got to the station in time to catch the next train into Loule. Jo and I had a fun time, hitting the Loule market, exploring a bit of the castle ruins, and then—heaven—going to a buffet restaurant with Chinese, Portuguese, and American choices. Bliss.

Jo dropped me back at the Loule station and I caught the train back. A full day and, with the extra walking from one train station to the main station, I was pretty much done in. When you get to a certain age, everything hurts for no reason. At least this time there was a good reason for all my joints to rise up in protest.

I tried to call an Uber and couldn't get the app to work. I figured it was a signal problem and hiked into town. (I was already at 17,000 steps for the day.) And I did get signal long enough to start the Uber process, but my GPS put me in the wrong place and the driver couldn't find me. I finally flagged down a taxi to get my sore and tired ass home.

Once home, I realized that my Portugal phone needed "topping off." It's a pay-as-you-go type phone and I get a certain number of talk and data minutes for ten or 20 Euros. I hadn't topped it off for a while because I was still getting WhatsApp messages, never thinking it was running off the Wi-Fi in my apartment. Oh, joy! More things you learn the hard way!

And really, this is how I learn a lot of things here. Not the smartest way to go, I'll admit, but it's weird little things you don't think about in your day-to-day life in the States.

If you are going to move to another country, please understand that at first, every day is a navigation. It's a new world and things work differently. Some better, some worse, almost all are different. There's a phrase in product development called

Least Viable Product (LVP). It's when a new product is released with very basic features and the final product is later released in a new and improved form after getting feedback from users. When I first arrived, and really for this first year, I operated at the LVP level. Just enough knowledge to get by and I added "new features" every day. Teeny, tiny, sometimes barely perceptible features.

I have learned to fake my way through various situations. On my walks, a simple *bom dia* gets me past most people. But there's a friendly lady who always adds something. Sometimes it's "How are you," which I can handle. One day it was something about her legs not working well. One day, she made a comment about the lady in front of me wearing earphones, who couldn't hear her friendly greeting. I think. She laughed and I laughed with her, hoping she wouldn't catch on to my lack of comprehension.

During the month I lived in Ohlão, I finally got brave and figured out how to use the ATMs. The first few times were a crapshoot. I figured out which button to press to get money out, and really, that's all I ever use ATMs for. But you're also able to pay bills with the machines and do all sorts of magical things. I have learned that when the person in front of you at the ATM has a sheaf of paperwork in their hands, it's a good idea to go get a *galão* (latte) and come back in 15 minutes.

At the grocery stores, I have learned that the cashier greets you and almost immediately asks if you need a sack. I had no idea what the words were, but I'd show them my sack when they said something and it's all good. (Eventually, I caught the word "*saco*." Duh.) They would ring up my purchases, tell me the amount, and I would pay with my debit card, having no idea how much I paid until I looked at the receipt. Since I could only buy as much as I could carry, I figured it couldn't be too bad and I was going to pay it anyway.

Looking back, I guess I learned not to have to know (yeah, control) every last thing; to just trust that most situations weren't life or death or financial suicide, and any mistake could be remedied. It all gets figured out. So yes, there are frustrations and a learning curve to the expat life. There are frustrations to life back in the US. Life is a continuous learning curve. ("Well, we won't do **THAT** again!")

But you know what I like? (Besides the pastries...)

I like that my brain has to work a bit harder here. I imagine I am building new neuro pathways as I attempt to learn the language. I have to figure something out almost every day. There's a lot to be said for living in your comfort zone. I mean, hey, it's a **COMFORT** zone. I get it. But there's also a point where comfort is stagnation. For many people, that's okay. But I've always been that kid who wanted to see what was going on outside of wherever I am.

There are so many things that I love about living here. There are also some days that are harder than others. If you understand that going in—and know that the good days increase as you go along—it makes the not-as-easy days easier. I have had only one or two days when I was ready to give the whole thing up, and even then, it wasn't the whole day. There's so much stuff in this world. So many things to learn. And so much fun to be had. A few blisters on my toes are a small price to pay.

Just as I had good days and bad days back in the States, I have them here. Four years in, I am still navigating certain things. New things, which means I am branching out. As I learned more of the language and the way things worked, I navigate this new life a bit more easily. And I am no longer having to navigate on a daily basis; I have built a comfort zone. People here are amazingly patient and helpful. I love where I am—the location, the pace, the scale. But I also know that if I'm not doing something new, I am not living this new life fully.

Chapter Sixteen

Building My Network

I Made a Friend!

I met my first local-to-Tavira friend and—proving life is random—he's in one of my Facebook writer groups.

While I was in Olhão, a man in a nonfiction writers' group joined and did the standard introductory post. He mentioned he lived near Tavira. I made the uncharacteristic move of suggesting a coffee meeting once I had made the move to Tavira. (I was being very brave. For me.) He was away for much of June, but in July, he suggested a place to meet up for coffee.

It's a bit strange meeting up with people you've never met in real life. I'm always afraid I won't recognize them or they won't recognize me and we'll miss the connection. I arrived a few minutes early, but John had already set up camp. He was at a table on the terrace with several of his research books spread around, and a beer in front of him. He had decided to get there early and get a bit of work done on his book.

John had that whole British, Hugh Grant, polite stammering thing down. Of course I was immediately charmed. I ordered a wine while he gathered up his papers and we started talking writing, then about our backgrounds, how we ended up in Portugal in general and Tavira in specifics. I am always afraid that I won't be able to keep up my end of the conversation, but when you meet up with someone you're naturally in sync with, the conversation is easy. I'd say it flows, but it really jumps back and forth, topic to topic and back again. He mentioned his partner several times. They had a son, and he had a daughter from a previous relationship. He was enormously proud of both of his kids.

I had done some basic stalking of him before meeting up, as one does... He had a degree in Psychology. He'd done an online certification with the Harvard Kennedy School. In England, he had been the director of a nonprofit, helping people with congenital heart defects. He was from Liverpool, which pulled all my Beatles strings. He was serious about his work and had the chops to back it up.

We talked about his book. He never directly said it, but he had grown up in a household with abusive parents. He had worked his way through it and his book was meant to help others get past neglectful or abusive childhoods. The wonderful thing I learned about John over the years was that he had found happiness and he wanted others to have it, too.

He didn't articulate it that way when we first met. It was something I saw as we talked over the years, as I watched him with his partner Catherine and his son Thomas. When I saw how absolutely thrilled he was whenever his daughter or brother came to visit. He loved these people and wanted them to know happiness, to experience it. He wanted them to be as happy as he was. I always say "Portugal isn't for everyone" but for the people who resonate with it, it goes deep.

I would like to say that John was the first of many friends here, but he was really the first of a treasured few, which now includes Catherine and Thomas. I have many acquaintances, but true friendships run deeper and they are rare.

Expats Need a Network

Just a few weeks after meeting John, the fact that expats need a network was brought home to me.

It was August. The fishing boats came in with their catches, each taking its turn at the pier. We had five days of hot, dry weather which finally broke. It was still warm, but there was enough of a breeze to keep things cool. I have no air conditioning in my apartment; most people here don't have air conditioning. The buildings are somehow built to stay cool in the summer. It would work against me in the winter—I planned on buying some space heaters by November, but, with the exception of one very hot day, it had been relatively comfortable. Or at least not too uncomfortable.

Summers are dry and hot in the Algarve and it has its share of wildfires every year. One Monday night, I watched a blanket of reddish smoke work its way across the sky. John and his family, in the hills on the other side of Tavira had to evacuate for the night. My friend, Jo, in Vilamoura messaged me that night asking if I needed a place to evacuate to. I was fine. The next night, a wildfire started near her home and she was the one preparing to evacuate; I returned her offer of a place to stay if needed. The *bombeiros* were out in full force and within a day or two, had put the fires out or had them in the "conclusion" stage. Like the American west, the fire danger is often at high alert in the summers.

Smoke from nearby fires darken the afternoon sky.

This is a village of brick and stucco and tile roofs. The fishermen's huts at the end of town are wood. I sat there on that night calculating how much of the town would actually burn if the fire made it here. I also tried to figure out what my evacuation plan would be since I don't have a car or any friends close by. Could I call an Uber? Maybe. I eyeballed the boats in the canal, trying to figure out how to wrap my laptop so it wouldn't get wet if I had to make a swim for it. (Note to self: Buy duct tape.)

When you move thousands of miles away on your own, you need to make contingency plans. You need to think about the what ifs: *What if I get COVID even though I'm vaccinated? What if I break a hip? What if my apartment burns to the ground?*

Fortunately, I have lived alone for most of my life. I know how to self-Heimlich. I keep a full dose of antibiotics in the fridge. I had someone I could call if something went horribly wrong, but I realized I should probably have several somebodies. I figured those somebodies would come in time. My contingency was that I could fly someone over to me if something truly dire happened. Not fast, but at least a back-up plan.

I am a self-contained unit, but I am also getting older and I know that shit happens, no matter how much you plan. Years ago, I read a funny line: If money can solve it, it's not a problem; it's a situation. To which I would often add, "Oh, boy, this is a big situation."

In Florida, we had hurricanes, but there is so much advance warning (and differing models of where any one hurricane is heading) that you take your time before packing a bag. Usually, you just go to the store to get more beer and snacky snacks. But tornados, earthquakes, and wildfires can arrive with no warning. A big advantage to moving 4,000 miles is that I have learned I don't need "all my things"—I can replace most of my stuff with a quick shopping spree at the local mall or just re-order from Amazon. I am much more clear on what is a necessity and what is just a comfort item. I am very sure I can pack a go-bag in under 10 minutes.

There are risks to everything we do. You run a certain amount of risk every time you drive your car to the grocery store. I took a risk moving to a country where I didn't know anyone. Do I feel isolated here? Yes, a little. As an introvert I am isolated everywhere, but I know that it takes on a different and riskier connotation when you're thousands of miles away from family and friends. Expats need a network.

That is why there are expat communities. That's why you need to learn the language and make friends with locals. People need networks for survival, even the self-contained units like me. I had lived in this small village for two and a half months. My Portuguese sucks. I am an introvert. But every morning I would take a walk and *bom dia* the hell out of everyone. I pet all the dogs (not to network, I just like dogs). I wave to the old men who sit on the benches by the pier. I talk to the man who works on his boat every morning and the ladies at the post office. I put a coin in the tip jar for the staff at the bakery who start bagging a croissant for me when they see me walk in.

And, it finally happened. As I took my walk one morning, the man who works on his boat drove by and honked and waved. The other day the lady who used to work at the bakery beeped at me from her scooter as she went to her new job. The men on the benches now wave and call out *bom dia*.

I was slowly building a network. The epidemic slowed me down quite a bit as far as networking in groups. Yes, there were some expat meetups, and even though I was vaxxed, I was leery of variants, especially since we were in high tourist season and people were coming in from all over. At the time, I passed on meeting up in any group of more than four people. I realized I needed my language skills to increase so I could meet and socialize with more locals. In the meantime, I kept up my daily walks and kept an eye on the wildfire map. I like to calculate my risks.

Chapter Seventeen

Festa, Bagels, and Possibilities

In August, it seems all of Europe goes on vacation. That's because EU countries mandate a minimum of four weeks' vacation a year (see how well that flies with your boss in the US), and kids' summer vacations are only about six weeks long. Everything gets jammed into August. COVID was, of course, affecting travel plans. People coming from outside the EU needed to be vaccinated and have a European vaccination certificate. Everyone flying needed to take a COVID test. People seemed to be more compliant with masking here than they were in the US, which made me feel safer. I had been vaccinated in July (with the one-shot J&J), but I was still keeping a wide berth when it came to holiday makers.

Santa Luzia is known as "The Octopus Capital of the World." The first time I saw a man walking down the street with an octopus in his hands, holding it like a bowling ball (candlepin, of course) with the tentacles hanging down, I flat-out gawked. Now, it's just a normal day.

During that summer, I thought a lot about the balance of tourist dollars vs. the spread of COVID. Tourism makes up about 20% of Portugal's GNI. 2020 had been a disaster for tourism, of course. 2021 was better but nowhere near what it had been in 2019. For Santa Luzia, many of the tourists are Portuguese, so the testing at the borders didn't affect it as much as maybe some of the bigger tourist areas. We all hoped that the Delta variant—the latest in COVID mutations—wouldn't kick up. If it did, travel restrictions between municipalities would be reinstated which would definitely have an effect on the towns that make their money in the summer months.

Festa Dos Pescadores

Santa Luzia's biggest festival, really, the festival it is known for, is Festa dos Pescadores. It's celebrated the second weekend in August. The festival had been canceled in 2020 due to COVID and people were looking forward to this year's festa, even if it was a little tamped down. The town was sprucing itself up: A new sign welcomed people to the village; public works people were repairing cobbles near the ferry landing, the tented kiosks were popping up in the park near the fishermen's huts. In the past, the kiosks lined the main street, from one end of town to the other, with a huge music stage set up at the opposite end from the fishermen's huts. While the 2021 festival was not as big, the procession from the church to the docks took place, with statues of saints surrounded by flowers being carried and the priest doing the traditional blessing of the fishermen and their boats. Instead of the huge soundstage, a flatbed truck circled the town with a different band for each of the three nights of the festival, people trailing behind it, partying in the open air. I had a front row seat from my balcony. It was as if the entire town was refusing to allow the pandemic to douse their spirit.

Most of the restaurants in Santa Luzia, the Airbnbs, even the beach vendors, make their money in the three and a half months of summer tourism. This year gave businesses just enough money to hang on and squeak through another year. But as I learned the back streets of the town, I saw restaurants that were closed and were likely not to reopen. Even a few on the front were closed. COVID had taken its toll on the local economy.

Now that I've found this spot, I want to keep it to myself. I know it's selfish and I know the people here have to make a living. Twelve (or more) hour workdays are the norm. Jobs are hard to come by. I won't begrudge the ten or so weeks a year when this village welcomes visitors, feeds them well, and then sends them back to their hotels. And in truth, the constant parade of people is now my favorite form of entertainment.

Knowing how fragile the local economy was, I made a conscious effort to spend more of my money in the town itself, rather than ordering from Amazon or going into Tavira. I started with the village markets.

As confusing as the bigger grocery stores were, the village store that I knew of (it turns out, there are several) was intimidating to me for a couple of reasons. First, the language barrier. I knew I couldn't count on anyone speaking English and it wasn't their job to speak English. Second, the stores are small and cramped, rabbit warrens with aisles so narrow that you sometimes have to turn sideways and back up against a shelf or case to allow another person through. It has two "main" aisles that meet at the butcher counter at the back of the store. But if you go through one of the two doorways that look like they are for employees only, there's an entire back section that's a jumble of assorted stuff, reminiscent of old-time general stores. The aisles back there are barely wide enough for one person and if you encounter another person, you simply back up and go the other way.

At first, it looks like a large storage room. It's organized to a certain extent—there's a cleaning supplies section and household goods area. Well, the household goods can be found anywhere back there, really. A few plumbing supplies are right next to the hair brushes and alcohol wipes. There's very little rhyme or reason to the back room and I never know what I will find there. One week it was the right size coffee filters that I couldn't find anywhere else (and still can't). Another time it was rubbing alcohol. There's what may be a very large mug or perhaps a small canister with a cheerful poop motif. Another one with smiley faces. I can get kitchen towels, panti-liners, and a new shower hose without moving more than a few steps. Even if I'm only stopping in for eggs and potato chips, I always check the back room. It's the equivalent of a treasure hunt with a better than 50/50 chance of finding something fun.

The butcher counter is small but has a surprisingly good supply of fresh meat and a real butcher. I ordered some chicken breasts and happened to turn around and glance at the bread rack. To my amazement, there were packaged bagels. Granted, they are from a commercial bakery, meaning processed, however they were real bagels and called out to me.

I asked the young man at the counter, who is more fluent in English than he knows, if they always had bagels. He explained that they didn't always get the same things in. As with the larger supermarkets, what you find here today you may not find again for weeks, if ever. That's okay. I don't need to be eating bagels every day. (Mostly because the bakery next door has fresh croissants every day...)

Unless you're in a tourist town, bagels are hard to find here. I mean bagels like you get at a bagel place in the States.

I'm not a huge bagel eater—it wasn't like I started off every day with a bagel. But they were "road trip" food and a quick, filling thing to grab when you were out running errands. Or just to enjoy on a lazy Saturday. So, when I found a bag of bagels at Costco in Seville, I was like, "YES, PLEASE!" Unfortunately, they were basically bread in the shape of a bagel. Even I, someone who should never be allowed in a kitchen, could tell that these things were never boiled, as a proper bagel should be. I ended up tossing the last few out. They were not worthy.

When I found a bag of bagels at the village store, I didn't get my hopes up. They turned out to be not bad—they had the right texture and even a bit of an eggy flavor. If they hadn't been boiled at some point, they had at least been chemically treated to make it seem so. I will not investigate that any further; some things are better left unknown. But after the disappointment I had with the Costco bagels, they were a nice treat; a taste of my old life in the States. (For the record, you can find Philadelphia cream cheese just about everywhere here.)

There are certain things I miss but I will not die without them. I'll probably be healthier without them, truth be told. In the expat groups, you often see people trying to find all the stuff they used to get in their home countries. There are British stores that stock items that British expats crave. (Tougher to stock after Brexit—between COVID lockdowns and Brexit, the Brits were not happy campers.)

At one point, I was on the hunt for confectioners' sugar. I was sure stores stocked it—I just hadn't figured out what it was called or how it was packaged. (Hot dogs come in glass jars here. Not refrigerated. And a really weird texture. Do **NOT** recommend!) I figured I would eventually trip over confectioners' sugar, just as I eventually found the real vanilla extract. Once I have found something, I can usually find it again because now I know what I'm looking for—the colors, the words, the packaging, but not the location in the store because that can change.

But there are some things that I will just not find. And that's okay. I am becoming familiar with Portuguese brands and I no longer stare at EVERY food item confused as to what it is or if it's going to taste weird. (It took me a while to trust the shelf-stable milk and cream; now I stock it on the regular.)

I was finding new favorites. I was finding the Portuguese equivalents to what I used to buy back in the States. Little by little, I was adjusting and growing more comfortable with the day-to-day.

You adapt or you go home. Or maybe you spend the rest of your life bitching that you can't find decent maple-flavored bacon or some convenience food that is jam-packed with chemicals. (I know—it's the chemicals that make it taste so good! I grew up with a Hostess Bakery in my town: I am the poster child for processed foods.)

I didn't move to Portugal to recreate my old life in a new country. Many people do. That's their thing and that's okay. With enough money, I suppose you can create your old life anywhere. But many people come here, are disappointed to find that the living is not incredibly cheap (it is less expensive, but not cheap), refuse to adapt, and spend the next several years bitching in expat groups until they leave, sometimes to a new place where they will eventually be equally unhappy.

I'm delighted I found bagels that taste similar to US bagels. I'm always happy when I find something that used to be a comfort food for me. (I ate a LOT of Oreos when I first got here.) But I'm more delighted when I try something new and find a new favorite.

Your favorite doesn't have to be your favorite forever. In fact, you can have LOTS of favorites. And, you don't have to be an expat to explore and find new cool stuff. You just have to make room in your life for possibilities.

Chapter Eighteen

I'm Somebody Now in Portugal!

September rolled around, and the relentless heat of August dropped a few notches to a perfect temperature.

September represented the last big hurdle in my immigration journey: My in-country appointment with SEF (now AIMA). The initial visa in my passport had been valid for four months, but it was extended through the end of the year due to all the COVID cancellations. This appointment was for my residency *permit*: The visa lets you in; the permit lets you stay. This was just one of the many, many things I didn't understand when I arrived in Portugal.

If you come into the country on a D7 visa, you need to be a resident of Portugal for five years before you can apply for citizenship. (That will be a whole 'nother process.) Your first residency permit is good for two years, then you have to renew, doing the paperwork all over again. Maybe. The government was streamlining processes, automating more of SEF's functions, and putting more processes online. Which is great, but right now, during the multi-year transition period, the way things will work two years from now is not quite set in stone.

To make it worse, when you ask in expat groups about people's experiences in their residency appointments, they are all different. (I swear!) The paperwork you need to have is pretty standard—SEF/AIMA has a list on their website and the list is also on the application form.

But according to the scuttlebutt in the expat groups, different offices will sometimes ask for all of the documents or only a few of the docs. You need to show €8,500 in your Portuguese bank account. No, you just need to show over €8,500 in assets. No, you just need to show reliable passive income of more than €8,500 a year. No, you need to show passive income *and* assets *in* Portugal. In some offices the clerks are fluent in English; in others they are not at all fluent. (Nor should they have to be.) Some of the appointments take 20 minutes or less, others take more than an hour. In a few of the locations, you need to bring two recent passport size photos. Others have cameras. Still others have the new biometric devices.

If you're an over-thinker like I am, conflicting information will make you more than a little crazy. I so wanted to get all this paperwork perfect. I was incredibly worried that after all the time, effort, and money I had put into getting here, they might kick me out. (Yes, of course I go directly to the worst-case scenario. Welcome to me.) I even worried about whether I should fill out the application in black ink or blue and came damn near to doing two, one in each color. I went with black ink. I'm fairly sure it wouldn't have mattered, but I'm still not completely sure.

Last-Minute Scramble

A few days before my appointment, someone in one of the groups reported that you now had to have €8,500 in a *Portuguese* bank account. I felt sick. I had a few thousand in there, but the balance of my money was scattered in different accounts in the States. And living in Portugal for almost nine months had cut into my limited savings a bit.

That started a mad scramble to move money into my Portuguese account. I had already obtained a statement from my bank attesting to the balance in my account. I managed to get all the necessary money deposited into my Portuguese account, but the letter I had showed a balance that was a few hundred euros short of what was necessary. I went online and printed out two copies of my bank statement with the new balance and hoped that would be enough.

The Residency Permit Appointment

I arrived hours ahead of my appointment and made sure I knew exactly where the office was. This was my first trip to Faro and I walked up to the Municipal Market carrying my bag of documents. My friend from Albufeira (she of the hair-dye request) met me for coffee and her cheerful chattering helped distract me from obsessing. I smiled and commented when appropriate, but my brain was racing. *What if my paperwork is wrong? What if they don't take my bank statement? What if they don't* like *me?*

It was junior high all over again.

I showed up to the appointment 15 minutes early. I didn't have to wait more than a few minutes. I had every piece of paperwork I could possibly need in my bag. In duplicate. I had the main folder with all the required paperwork from the list, a second "in case they ask" folder, and a third "if weirdness happens" folder. And an extra blouse in case I spilled something on my shirt before the appointment. I was READY.

And the appointment went as smooth as silk. The agent was very kind, fluent in English, and professional. The Faro office is very up-to-date and had the new biometric ID set up. He obviously had all my original paperwork from the visa application and asked for very little additional paperwork. The main things he seemed to need were my passport, visa, and NIF (finance number). He did ask if I had a utente (healthcare) number. I explained I couldn't get one without a residency permit but I had a temporary one that I got for my vaccine. I volunteered that I have private health insurance. He nodded, unconcerned, and didn't ask for any of that paperwork. My original visa application had the required paid year of health insurance. (God forbid anyone would have to actually access it—I'm very sure it was crap.)

He never asked for my Portuguese bank statement.

But you can bet if the money wasn't in there, he would have. This I know deep in my heart.

He scanned documents, he stamped things, I signed things. He took my picture (three tries, bless him), my fingerprints, and I think they did some sort of body scan, so I'm pretty sure they know what my BMI is. (Kidding. I hope.) I paid around €150 for the permit and I was told I'd receive my biometric card in the mail sometime in the next month or so. The appointment took about 45 minutes. And two weeks of pure angst.

I received a piece of paper that declared I was now a resident. The laminated card, when I received it, would make it even more official. I walked out of the office and went down to the main floor of the Market before breaking into a dance. Okay, not a full-on dance, but there was a bit of jumping about in the ladies' room.

I felt like Steve Martin in The Jerk.

I was now officially a legal resident of Portugal. I had somehow blundered my way through the paperwork properly and made it through the two most anxiety-ridden weeks of my Portuguese life. Moving here had been a series of steps, made a little more difficult by COVID.

But I'm a real person now!

I managed not to say that out loud, in case you're wondering. But the smile on my face stretched some muscles I hadn't used in a while.

Big Exhale

Now, I could breathe. I had been in limbo for almost nine months, waiting for this appointment. I didn't know what to expect and honestly, up until a few weeks before, still wasn't clear on the requirements for the permit. Actually, while I was confident I had what I needed when I walked into the appointment, I also knew that weirdness could happen. But I had done all I could, tried to plan and prepare for every contingency. From what I'd heard in the groups, if something wasn't right in your paperwork, they told you to fix it and made a new appointment for you. While I was fairly sure I wouldn't be escorted to the border if something was wrong, I wanted to get it right the first time. New appointments were months in the future and subject to change. I wanted to finally feel settled.

And I did. I had my long-term apartment. My Wi-Fi was reliable. I was learning more about the area where I lived. With COVID restrictions relaxing (85% of the country was fully vaccinated at this point), and my permit in hand, I felt like I was finally free to explore more of my new home.

As Steve Martin said in *The Jerk*, "Things are going to start happening to me now!"

Chapter Nineteen

You Meet All Sorts

Some days I just like to have a wander. The town of Tavira has a farmers' market, which is not huge compared to some, but big enough for me, particularly because I don't really eat vegetables or fruit. Or fish. I mean, I do eat some fruits and veggies (not fish though), but I don't get excited by perfect little eggplants or... really I can't even remember the fruits and veggies that were there. I remember a lot of chestnuts, olives, and... other things? Lots of local honey.

I was happy to just wander through, looking at everything, because really, if you like fruits and veggies and olives, and fish, it is a wondrous place—colors, sounds. Not the smells so much because... fish. Beside the mercado is a weekly flea market with something for everyone—lots of china and glassware, jewelry, coins, the dribs and drabs of household detritus that you find at every flea market. And a lovely cacophony of people speaking at least six different languages.

And if you're asking, "Did you take any pictures, Barb?" I have to admit that no, I did not. Partly it's a privacy issue—it's considered rude to take people's pictures and use them without permission. Mostly it's because I never think to take pictures until it's too late. I have gone on two-week vacations and come home with four pictures, all of them blurry and poorly composed. I am a words girl. Sigh.

I'm going to tell you this next story in real time, hoping you can experience just a bit of the surrealness of the encounter.

I wander the flea market, but I don't buy anything because then I would have to carry whatever I bought around all day and I have a few more stops to make. The first stop is the Irish pub, The Black Anchor, set on the other side of the river Gilão that runs through Tavira. They are having a book sale for charity and I figure there will be English language novels in the mix.

I find the pub and walk in, trying to look like I know where I am going and what I am doing. I'm sure I look as uncertain and out of place as I feel. New is sometimes hard, especially when you're by yourself. And, as an introvert, I am really not good about asking strangers for directions or help. I look around the first little section of the pub (football on all screens, of course), don't see any books so I keep walking through to what looks like other seating areas. I find a few tables of books set up in a back corridor and happily start nosing through. I hit upon three thick novels to keep me occupied (at least one of which

I have read before), spot a donation bucket, and put in every coin I have. I have that bad foreigner habit of not thinking of coin euros as the equivalent of American folding money which works to the advantage of donation boxes, kids raising funds for school trips, and restaurant servers. One of the servers sees me with my books and says she, too, has bought a book. Another reader.

I walk outside and choose a table, happy to settle in the sunshine with my books and the prospect of a pub lunch. I order a glass of red wine and a cheeseburger with crispy steakhouse chips (because potatoes *are* one of my vegetables), and learn the European Portuguese word for crispy which is different from the Brazilian Portuguese word for crispy. (I am learning the important words first.) My server is from Brazil and we first chat about the differences between Brazilian and European Portuguese and then about the books we have bought. She has bought a book titled *The Customer is Always Wrong*, a saga about an artist working as a waitress in 1970s Oakland, California. We laugh about the title. We both have found little treasures.

My wine arrives and I sit in the sun, absorbing the day. As shy as I am about approaching someone for help, I have no problem dining alone; I've been doing it for decades. Another older, single lady comes and sits at the table next to me. She strikes up a conversation in heavily accented English and I think, *"Aha! The expat experience of meeting interesting people while dining at an outdoor café! THIS is why I came to Europe!"*

The Black Anchor with the "Roman" Bridge in the background.

She asks where I am from and when I say the United States, she exclaims, "Of course, you are from the United States. I can tell by your accent. I have lived in the United States. What part?" But she doesn't really listen to the answer. She was born in Paris, but she is Russian and her grandfather was the greatest dancer who ever lived.

I sip my wine. She insistently flags down the server who politely asks if she would like a menu. "Of course, I want a menu. I am here to eat!" My eyebrows twitch. She orders a gin and tonic and peruses the menu.

"When you are a woman, alone, it is hard to get noticed," she explains.

I agree. Women become invisible at a certain age. But, I also recognize that service is leisurely here and usually a simple wave of your hand or nod of your head will catch the server.

She tells me "I don't eat, but I am drinking so I need to have food." She goes on to tell me that one time she didn't eat for three months because she has learned some sort of meditation technique in India where you no longer need food. But today she is eating because she is drinking. Otherwise, of course, she wouldn't bother with food. I get the distinct impression that food is beneath her.

She is traveling to Thailand and Goa and somewhere else over the next few weeks. She used to be a journalist (a common past profession among expats—I think it means something different here than it does in the US). Her grandfather, it finally comes out, was the dancer Nijinski. I have to agree, yes, he was the greatest dancer in the world. He was also Polish, not Russian, but I felt that little tidbit of information was not going to help the conversation. She had a wonderful American grandmother (must have been from the other side—Nijinski married a Hungarian). I mention Anna Pavlova. She was a contemporary. Did they dance together?

She brushes over the question. "Well, yes. Of course. Pavlova." She keeps chattering but she has faded a bit. She pauses her monologue—briefly—to ask what I do. I'm a writer, I say. Business books. My food arrives.

"Ah, my parents were both writers. They published many books. When I was 14, I wrote a novel and that was published."

I marvel at her accomplishment—a published novel at 14! Encouraged, she proceeds to outline the novel she had written. How mature she was to write a novel with that theme, she observes of her younger self. She comes from a family of artists. She played the violin, learning from the age of three or four. Her brother and sister were very jealous of her but she had to practice four hours a day. That was very hard on a small child. No one in her family is a dancer; it was not allowed. There is no reason given for this.

I let her chatter as I eat. I very much like when someone carries the conversation so I can chow down.

She doesn't spend very much money, she says. She bought her Christian Dior handbag at the thrift shop for three euros. Her jeans and shoes for a euro or two. She goes to the flea markets. She has €100,000 at her disposal that her children urge her to spend, but what does she need?

Her food comes. She is very skilled at eating and speaking at the same time, without once opening her mouth with food in it. I wonder if they teach you how to do that at finishing school, but she hasn't mentioned going to one yet (though I'm fairly sure it would have been in Switzerland and quite exclusive).

She lived and worked in Chicago. She did interviews for Playboy magazine in the 60s. She met all the right people. She seduced that minister in the Kennedy administration. (I'm thinking, Kennedy administration?? Take your pick in that crowd.) She excuses herself, leaving her purse on the table. Comes back with a cigarette and lights it.

"I don't smoke, but sometimes..."

I nod. I tell her that by the seventh week of working on a ship in Mexico, even I, a non-smoker, would occasionally indulge. We talk a bit about Mexico. She says she used to live there, on the Pacific side. I say the ship I worked on traveled the Baja peninsula, the Pacific and Sea of Cortez. I mention Cabo San Lucas. She says she lived farther south. She's talking mainland Mexico because you can't go farther south than Cabo on the peninsula. I don't say this to her, but I obviously know too much about Mexico. Time to change the subject.

She blows out a stream of smoke. "Kissinger. I seduced Kissinger."

I laugh. "Well, that's not very hard. He was pretty easy."

She is taken a bit off her stride. I soften it.

"Kissinger loved women." I add, "He was in the Nixon administration, not Kennedy." I am thinking the men in the Kennedy administration were at least better looking. "I think he is still alive," I add.

She nods but I can tell she is disappointed that I am not impressed. (But I mean, really? Kissinger? He slept with everybody.)

She has been married four times. But never divorced. Her last husband died because she could not speak Portuguese to explain to the people at the hospital that he couldn't stand up. I don't know why she didn't ask her husband to try to stand to demonstrate the problem. I don't give voice to that thought, either. They sent him home and he died. She doesn't feel guilty, because she doesn't feel guilty about anything, guilt is useless, but she feels like if she could only have told them, he might have lived. But the people at the hospital didn't speak English or French. She speaks both languages but refuses to learn Portuguese.

"I am 85 years old." (I protest, feigning shock. Because that is expected.) "I speak two languages. I am not going to spend my time learning this difficult language."

I can understand that from an age and years left standpoint. I nod. Portuguese is difficult.

"How long have you lived in Portugal?" I ask.

"Five years."

I tell her, "I am a resident here so I am working to learn the language."

She tells me she speaks supermarket Portuguese—enough to get by but can't be bothered with actually learning more. I don't point out the obvious—if she had learned a bit more in those first three years, maybe her husband wouldn't have died. Or maybe he would have but she would have known that he could not be helped.

She excuses herself. "Two minutes." Then she is back.

She has a boyfriend. He is 20 years her junior, wealthy and handsome. He's so handsome that people are surprised when they meet him. She is insulted. Do they think she would have an ugly boyfriend? But all he really talks about is football. Men are so tedious with their sports, she says. I understand, I say, sipping the last of my wine.

She is in touch with her first husband—they are still friends. My mind connects back to her statement that she has never divorced. Makes those next three marriages suspect. I say nothing. This is her story.

It is time to ask for the check. She insistently flags down the server and asks for the check using the Spanish word. I ask using the Portuguese word. Or at least the European Portuguese word. My server is Brazilian but of course, she knows. Earlier we had talked about the language differences. She brings our checks. I catch her eye and say, "That book you bought? I think you bought the right one." My eyes slide over to the woman at the next table. She laughs and agrees.

Now the woman is searching through her small Christian Dior bag. "I don't think I have any money with me."

"That could be a problem," I say, unsympathetically. Not my first rodeo.

She keeps digging. "Ah, here it is."

Miraculous.

I gather my things.

"Let me get your number," she says. "It's so hard to find people to talk to."

"I only have a US phone," I lie, apologetically.

"No problem. I have WhatsApp."

Eeesh. I reluctantly give her my number, debating if I should give her the wrong one. I am not fast enough and give her the right one. We trade names.

"We can maybe get together."

"Ah, but you're traveling over the next few weeks," I remind her.

"Oh yes. After."

We part ways. I let her get ahead of me and intentionally take a different route, not knowing or caring if it adds extra steps and time to my trip. It's a wandering day and I wander on.

Chapter Twenty

My First Holidays in Portugal

While the Portuguese do not start putting out Christmas decorations in September (I'm looking at *YOU* every big box retailer in the States), the holidays were inching up and Thanksgiving was just around the corner.

I've been missing from family Thanksgivings and Christmases for much longer than I ever participated in them. Over the years since I moved away from my hometown, I've gone back for a few, one or the other, never both in the same year. Thirty years ago, when I worked on ships, I think I missed five years in a row of both holidays.

I have had lonely holidays and not-so-lonely holidays and holidays with lonely people. I've done the "orphan" Thanksgivings. I've done Thanksgivings with elderly relatives eating a Boston Market turkey dinner while we reminisced about holidays past with 20 or more gathered around a table groaning with homemade food.

Kids grow up and people scatter. They start new families and new traditions. People die and take their recipes with them. The table sometimes gets smaller.

The year my mother died, one of my longest-time friends and her husband came down to stay with me at Christmas—a kindness that did not go unnoted. This year, her mother passed but we are 4,000 miles apart and I cannot return the favor on the holiday. If the fates are willing, we will make up the lost time.

This year I am in a country that doesn't celebrate Thanksgiving. I know three English-speaking people, all Brits. I didn't know anyone here who celebrated Thanksgiving and that was okay—different country, different holidays.

I decided to go into Tavira to the Black Anchor. Once you've been somewhere, you feel more comfortable going back. I was pretty sure I wouldn't run into the crazy Russian/French/who knows lady again. However, I knew they had turkey on the menu. I thought ordering a turkey dinner on what was for everyone else just another Thursday would be mildly amusing to me. My little secret. But when I got there, I really wanted a cheeseburger and fries. After a short but lively debate carried out by the voices in my head, that's what I ordered. I sat in the sun, eating my burger and enjoying a glass of wine and I was pretty much content. No need for turkey.

A friend of mine in the States spent his Thanksgiving at a large family gathering of in-laws. He made himself useful cooking the turkeys, then spent the rest of the day making small talk, watching the games, and drinking steadily.

He can be polite; he's quite skilled at making small talk in social situations (I'm out after three minutes). He understands the social necessity of playing the amiable in-law. It's part of being in a relationship; part of being in community. If you know him, you can watch him chat with someone and see the restlessness in his eyes. Check the direction of his feet and they are pointed towards the nearest door. The person he is talking to has no idea that he is finding a way to excuse himself politely.

He was one of the friends who checked up on me later that day to see if I had "gotten my turkey." It's interesting (to me) that friends and family feel a little sad for you when they find out you didn't eat the traditional meal, which is code for "spent the holiday alone." When I told him I'd had a burger and fries he unknowingly summed up his holiday: "There's something to be said for having what you want."

Society and relationships (which build society) require us to give sometimes. Enduring eight hours of polite conversation, side stepping landmines with your partner's family (and for many people, even your own family) is one of those gives. Maybe that's what the "give" in Thanksgiving really means.

There's a reason why people have more stress and suicides go up in holiday season. It's not just the pressure of more to do and the impossible goal of perfection that Currier and Ives and every Hallmark Christmas movie set out for us.

I think part of it is the sameness of the experience: Every year you hear your sister-in-law snipe about your brother. You bite your tongue while your idiot uncle mansplains... well, anything. You are painfully reminded of whatever mistake you made as a kid and you laugh along with everyone thinking *for f*cks' sake, let it go.* (That's the sake of many f*cks.) Everyone participates in the tiptoeing around whatever elephant sits at the table uninvited.

The sameness is cumulative. It wears on us. It makes us wonder if things will ever change. Is that all there is? Is this how the rest of my life plays out?

We somehow have come to believe that holiday family meals and perhaps even office parties are required, not truly a voluntary gathering.

But people do choose to attend. Sometimes it's not onerous at all—it's an event looked forward to and enjoyed. Maybe people find comfort in the sameness. The shared times reinforce the relationships; the gatherings build traditions. Other times, attendance is a token of love or respect. Some would like to attend but are unable due to geography or economics. And some choose not to attend, either gracefully with a socially acceptable and plausible lie or less gracefully, with great drama and years of built-up hurt.

We make choices all the time. Some are small: "I'll have the burger, please." Some are life changing: "I'm moving to Europe."

One thing leads to another and another and another. Sometimes we watch the dominoes of our life fall with a detached curiosity. Many people are passive victims: "It's the way of the world. What can I do about it?" That's a choice.

Some see the dominoes fall and decide to change their course. They catch on to the pattern, see which domino they can move out of line soonest, and stop the chain reaction.

We make choices. Some of those choices put us in a box. Some free us up. Some of us make choices we might initially regret and, if we're lucky, at some point after that, we're glad we made it. The decision to start my own business at the age of 22 instead of moving into a "real career" was one that took a long time to feel confident about. It led to a lifetime of entrepreneurial ventures, some good, some not so good. But it also led to a lifetime of experiences and adventures that I never would have had if I had opted for a "good job with benefits." A thing that many people of my generation saw evaporate in front of their eyes. It led to me being free to work from anywhere in the world. I didn't know that would be the result of a decision made 40 years ago. Yet here I sit in Portugal, my fingers on the keyboard.

Sometimes the choice is made for us which is a nicer way to frame not having a choice. I guess I think mostly of a few old "loves" when I say this, who did not choose me. I might have been heartbroken at the time, but looking back, I can clearly see that we would have been a very bad combination. More than that, I can truly say I love seeing old boyfriends with the person who is the right choice for them.

Life flexes. A bad decision today could be rectified by a good decision tomorrow. That wall of your box that you hit face first at the holidays might not even be noticeable the rest of the year. Maybe the walls of your box grow farther apart as the years pass. Your box gets bigger; you run up against the walls less often. Sometimes the walls make you feel safe. Sometimes the walls close in.

Everyone's box is different. It can be your cubicle at a job you hate but need (right now). It can be the micro-economy that you built by starring in a hit TV show. If you quit, if you fail, a hundred people lose their jobs and unlike the stars, they don't have millions of dollars in the bank and a fistful of offers. You can have a luxury box with walls that are so beautifully decorated people don't even know they are walls. But you do.

Within those boxes we build our own walls. We are our own labyrinth. It can be hard to find your way out. We get turned around, confused, have decision fatigue, choose the path of least resistance because some days, just surviving on this dangerous planet takes everything we have.

But the walls we build we can also tear down. We can uncheck the box we put ourselves in, if not immediately, we can at least start the reversal.

The choice is yours. I made my choices. They all had upsides and downsides. But I am happy. I think that's a pretty big thing in this world.

Chapter Twenty-One

You Are Now Free to Move About Europe

My official, laminated residency permit arrived as promised, 30 days after my SEF appointment. Having it meant I could now safely travel outside of Portugal. You are only permitted two entries into Portugal on your residency visa and I, like everyone, had used one just by entering the country initially. This limitation isn't usually an issue—the visa is for four months and by then, you should have had your SEF appointment and been approved for the residency permit. But COVID had upended everything. People on visas were quite literally stuck in Portugal, not because they couldn't leave, but because they couldn't get back *in* on their visa—they'd already gone out once for whatever reason.

I had been over to Spain once, but no one was checking passports or visas at the border. Both Portugal and Spain are part of the Schengen Zone (and yes, the EU) and people can usually pass from country to country the way we pass through states. During the heaviest of COVID breakouts, the borders between countries were "closed" meaning there were passport checks and more important, you had to have a good reason to be traveling between countries. With the travel restrictions lifting and my residency permit in place, I was now free to travel out of Portugal. Yes, I needed to keep track of how many days I spent outside the country, but a two-week trip to Italy wasn't going to put too much of a dent in my out-of-country allowance.

One of the reasons I moved to Portugal was to have a base that gave me easy access to exploring all of Europe. My first real trip out of the country was checking off an item that had been on my bucket list for decades: Italy.

Mary Anne had offered to come over to spend the holidays with me. She is very kind-hearted and I know she didn't want me to spend my first Christmas in Portugal alone—even if I'm not religious. She and our friend Angie were taking a trip to Ireland, then Italy, and Portugal. Did I want to join them for the Italian part of the tour and we'd all come back to Portugal together, using my place as a base? Yes, please and thank you!

Mary Anne and Angie spent a week in Ireland and I flew over to Rome to meet up with them. I was very excited: This (THIS!)

was why I moved to Portugal! I felt like I was finally stepping into the picture I had of myself as a world traveler.

Visiting Italy had been on my bucket list for as many years as living in Europe had been. It is the country of my paternal grandparents. It is a place that has been a symbol of history and romance and yes, cute Vespa scooters and Audrey Hepburn in *Roman Holiday.*

Mary Anne did all the heavy lifting on finding accommodations in each of the cities we would visit. She had done multiple trips to Europe while this was Angie's first time. It was my first time in Italy and I was happy just to tag along.

I decided to emulate Mary Anne who is able to travel for a month with just a backpack and a personal bag. She had a travel capsule wardrobe that washes and dries quickly and easily. She is excellent at finding multiple uses for things.

I bought a backpack from Amazon Spain, my first ever. (Yeah, I'm a late-stage Boomer. What can I say?) I had this vision of me traveling Europe: I would be a no luggage, backpack kind of girl, swinging on and off planes and out of taxis with my hands free. [Cue Music: Georgy Girl] No long waits at baggage claim for me. If I am going somewhere and need more than my backpack, I am bringing TOO. MUCH. STUFF.

I packed what I needed for the two-week trip in my backpack (knowing there would be washing machines in the Airbnbs). I fit in my laptop, cords, adapter, even a few paper files. I used my cute packing cubes; they keep things organized, containing and compressing the rolled-up clothes I have jammed inside them. I remembered to put my liquid stuff into a little baggy and pack it on top.

It turns out, I can fit everything I need for a two-week trip into a backpack. But it's not about volume, boys and girls. It's about weight.

What weighed the backpack down is my laptop. It's not super heavy—in fact, it is balanced on my lap for about eight hours a day, no problem. But once it is in my backpack it suddenly doubles and triples in weight. (I may be exaggerating just a teeny bit.) Not a big deal as I caught my plane out of Faro.

When I landed in Rome, I was a bit disoriented by the sheer size of the airport. It was also the first airport I'd ever been in that didn't smell like Subway sandwiches. The Rome airport smells good, mostly because of all the upscale stores and perfumeries in their duty-free area.

I traipsed through to the exit, wondering if I was supposed to check in with immigration. I followed signs to the exit, figuring I'd get stopped at the appropriate place. Nope. I was going from one EU country to another. No fuss, no muss.

My driver had texted me and we went back and forth a bit until we found each other. We sped from the airport into the center of Rome and as we neared my Airbnb, I saw the Coliseum looming. Breath-taking.

I'd been texting with Mary Anne and they came out to meet me as I pulled up. My first words to her after not seeing her for 11 months: "Do you have a five euro note?" She didn't even blink. She handed it over, I tipped the driver and we headed up to the apartment. (Yes, I paid her back.)

We dropped my backpack in the room I was sharing with Angie and went out to find something to eat. I was thrilled to see an Irish pub just around the corner. If worse came to worse, I could get some pub food. Mary Anne and Angie, having just come from Ireland, were slightly less thrilled.

Italy, as well as the rest of the world, was still in heavy COVID protection. Many people wore masks, even outdoors. I had gotten used to not masking outdoors when walking around my little village. I masked up here out of courtesy and caution.

Restaurants asked to see your vaccine certificates before allowing you entry. It was chilly, but we leaned more towards outdoor dining. The restaurant we chose had lovely heaters set up and we were quite comfortable. The waiter was charming, the wine generously poured and the food delicious. We were sitting IN ROME eating a wonderful dinner under the stars. I couldn't believe I was finally in Italy!

Walking in Rome

Mary Anne had arranged a walking tour of the city for our first full day in Rome. Nina, our guide is a Rick Steves guide who had seen her work virtually disappear due to COVID and the dearth of tourists. We met her at the site of the Ludus Magnus, the gladiator training grounds, near the Coliseum. A transplanted American, she was personable and lovely and fun.

She loves Italy—all of it: the country, the history, the language, the culture—and it shows. I could not believe our good fortune in finding such a guide, but of course, it was really Mary Anne's doing. I think she is part witch and that works for me.

We explored the Coliseum, looking at the gates, hearing the history. Nina pointed out things that we would surely miss on our own. As we looked at the Arch of Constantine, Nina explained that this was one of only three remaining original arches, pointing out the sections that were "borrowed" from elsewhere which gave context to the economics of that particular period. At every stop, she expertly weaved in the changes that occurred over time, the politics that were behind the structures, the daily life of the people at the time.

The history is told in story format and she made it come alive. We walked around the "back" of the Coliseum (I mean, it's round—does it really have a back?) and learned about Palatine Hill, one of the famed seven hills of Rome. Everywhere I looked there were huge, gorgeous statues, more gates and arches, and of course, people snapping pictures of EVERYTHING, including, of course, themselves.

We stopped for a warming cappuccino at a spot not far from our Airbnb and then the tour continued on past archeological digs, monuments, and more modern areas. At Trajan's Column, we admired the carvings that curl around the column like a scroll, leading up to a statue of St. Peter at the top. Wait! Who? Frankly, we wouldn't have known who was standing up there or what we were looking at. Nina filled in that the carvings depict

Trajan's victorious campaigns against the Dacians. A statue of Trajan had originally topped the column but it disappeared in the Middle Ages and was later replaced by a statue of St. Peter. I suspect the original statue is hidden in a vault somewhere deep in the Vatican, but that's just me.

We moved on through the city streets. We saw the exact balcony where Mussolini gave a speech. We had specifically asked to go to the Jewish Ghetto, a Jewish enclave that was established in 1555. When Italy surrendered to Nazi Germany in September of 1943, almost 8,000 Italian Jews were in Rome. Within weeks, the Nazis demanded a payment of 50 kilograms of gold from the Jewish community, threatening to deport 200 family heads if the payment wasn't made. Payment was made by the deadline, just two days later. Less than three weeks after that, the Nazis raided the Jewish Ghetto, detaining 1,259 people. Of those, 1,035 were sent to Auschwitz. Only 16 survived.

Nina pointed out the "stumbling stones"—brass markers at the houses of Holocaust victims who were taken from their homes. It was hard to hold back the tears.

There was no fresh water available in the ghetto in the early days, and people had to get their water from a few fountains. We went to the "turtle fountain" at Piazza Mattei. There's also a cat sanctuary nearby and some subterranean ruins (all of Rome has subterranean ruins, really). This is, allegedly, where Caesar was stabbed. We stood in awe in front of a huge church, but didn't go in. We preferred not to go in most places, even with masks.

The tour finished and Nina left us, but not before pointing out some trusted restaurants. We wandered some more, waiting for restaurants to reopen. We had a wonderful early dinner at a restaurant in the ghetto. I, of course, ordered something safe. Mary Anne and Angie were more adventurous eaters. We walked back to our Airbnb, exhausted but happy.

The Vatican, Of Course

Of course, we did the Vatican Museum, which starts you off with rather mundane items with no context as you walk around the lobby. We wound our way through, the first displays within reach and therefore touchable. (We quickly ascertained that the "touchable" items were castings and not priceless artifacts as represented.) The deeper into the museum we went, the more valuable (and out of reach) the items on exhibit. We went upstairs and down stairs, moved into side galleries and through galleries. All of it, of course, leading to the ultimate goal of every visitor: the Sistine Chapel.

Going through the galleries that came before arriving at the Sistine Chapel was overwhelming. Most of the artwork is incredible; things you have read about and seen in books. A few pieces had us tilting our heads and asking, "What were they thinking?" Then you entered the hush of the Chapel. No photography is allowed in there and people are asked not to speak (or use hushed tones) so that everyone can take it all in. It is a lot to take in. And I kind of wished I had binoculars or a zoom camera lens to see the artwork a little better. Next time.

Just one section of the Sistine Chapel ceiling.

The galleries we went through after visiting the Sistine Chapel held a ***LOT*** of gold and jewels. It seemed like any one piece could fund someone or several someones for the rest of their lives. The amount of wealth in one place was almost stomach-turning. By the end of it, all I could think was that the Vatican could wipe out poverty by selling off a few bits and bobs. Seriously. For some reason they choose not to. Just sayin.

Is it stunning? Yes, of course. It made me wonder what other cool stuff they might have locked up in the vaults. It is wealth overwhelm, to be honest. I think of all the dimes and quarters I put in the collection plate on Sunday mornings and I can only shake my head. Well, at least I know where it ended up.

We caught a taxi back to our accommodations. How much? Twenty-seven euros. We chipped in and I handed it to the driver. "No, I said 37 euros." (As if the 27 wasn't overcharging enough.) He shortchanged me. I was pissed. I am sure he thought it was funny to take advantage of stupid American tourists. It left a bad taste in our mouths. We cleared it out later that night.

Mary Anne had decided her mission for this trip was to find the best carbonara in Italy—a worthy goal. I have NEVER had carbonara. Why? Because I am afraid there will be something in there I don't like. (Did I mention I have the eating habits of a spoiled three-year-old?) The restaurant we went to is actually called "Carbonara." It is small, with a chalk board menu, and truly charming staff. Mary Anne explained to me what is in carbonara—nothing scary, as it turned out—and I have found a new favorite dish. We don't know it yet, but this first carbonara will be the winner of the best carbonara contest.

Florence

Our next city was Florence and we packed our belongings up. My backpack was heavier than when I started because Mary Anne and Angie had brought me pounds(!) of Peets's coffee. I was definitely NOT going to complain about the extra weight.

We walked up to the train station, navigating with Google maps and going, as we do, in the general direction. The train station is huge and confusing. Angie and I were pretty useless at figuring out how to get tickets and where to find the trains. We walked up to one of the information counters. The woman there was very eager to help us out, so much so that we were afraid we were going to miss our train. She chattered on, telling us all about everything: what we should do in Rome, where we should go in Florence. Did you ever just stand there and watch words continuously fall out of someone's mouth? That was the three of us, trying very politely to explain that we just needed to be directed to where we could buy tickets. Mary Anne quietly disappeared, asked someone else, and led us to the ticketing machines. We took some time figuring out the machine, feeding in our money, and eventually, we all had tickets. We made our way to the platform and settled into our seats on the train, laughing about the chattiness of the information lady. She was definitely the right person for the job.

High speed trains get the job done. We went through rolling hills and in just a couple of hours, we were pulling into Florence, another madhouse of a train station. I was in dire need of coffee and even though there were several cafés in the station, they were crowded and we decided to get to our lodgings first.

I was *pretty* sure that our taxi driver had brought us to the wrong place when we pulled up outside our next Airbnb. A plaque on the building said "Embassy of Bangladesh" and I was **very** sure we didn't have diplomatic credentials. At least I didn't. We were in the right place but it was no longer an embassy. Or maybe just the bottom floor was the embassy? We loaded up our luggage and one person into the cubicle of a lift and two of us took the stairs. We were a bit early for check-in (the cleaners were still there) but able to drop off luggage, which freed up our hands to eat lunch.

By mere chance and good fortune, and the kind of coincidence that makes you feel like the universe is having a mischievous day, the restaurant kitty-corner from the embassy was one Mary Anne had visited and loved during a trip 30 years before. The food was still marvelous and stumbling upon this happy memory made it even more delightful. (Angie and I immediately noticed the Irish pub nearby. We saved that knowledge for the night we would be jonesing for a cheeseburger and fries.)

The Airbnb apartment itself was rather stunning. Fourteen-foot ceilings, marble floors, archways between the living and dining areas. The living room was big enough to hold a dance in. Even though the weather was grey (off-season has its downsides), there was plenty of light during the day because of the huge windows. In short, they were pretty swanky digs. Oddly, some of the amenities were not up to super-host standards. The owners seemed particularly concerned that people would steal their towels. (Trust me, the towels were not worth stealing.) They also gave us two rolls of toilet paper (one in each bathroom) for our three-day stay. With three women. And two hotel-size bars of soap. Nevertheless, we made ourselves at home. (And bought more toilet paper the next day.) The owners/managers were not nearly as helpful as most Airbnb super-hosts are. The place was spectacular; how the owners made it to super-host status we have no idea. The detailed instructions on what we needed to do upon departure only confirmed our dislike of the hosts.

The Duomo Area

We spent our first full day in Florence exploring the Duomo area, hitting into little shops, snapping pictures (do we still "snap" pictures?), and basically just feeling the vibe of the city. Florence has a most excellent vibe. For the first time in months, I heard American accents. Right out of the gate, we met a couple of American women, walking their dog. Cooing over dogs is a great way to meet people, but mostly, we just wanted to pet ALL the dogs. Angie and Mary Anne were missing their four-legged fur babies and Florence's dogs were happy to accept all the pats, back scratches, and reassurances that they were, indeed, such good dogs. I firmly believe dogs are polyglots and they all know "Who's a good doggie?" in every language.

Mary Anne had told me about the Fabriano Boutique, a wondrous shop with all kinds of incredibly fine paper and journals and pens and folders and all sorts of things that fascinate people who write and make art. Exquisite is the short review. Let's just say that if you are a writer, if you appreciate creamy paper and ink that flows from a pen effortlessly, the Fabriano Boutique is a must-shop.

We wandered into a leather goods store with a lovely elderly shopkeeper who insisted that we not look at the price tags; he would make us a happy price. And he did. There's nothing like breathing in the scent of leather; it is, to me, more intoxicating than any perfume. (Is that weird?) I found a gorgeous leather jacket, just the right weight for Portugal and Italy, at a price that made me not just happy but ecstatic. We stopped at several leather goods stores throughout the day, but ended up going back to "our" shopkeeper to buy gloves and a few more items. I am still thinking about marrying him.

I had two requirements for a lunch establishment: It must have something I would actually eat and it had to have HEAT. Again, off-season in Italy is chilly and damp. We had a fantastic lunch in the backroom of a little restaurant, splitting a pizza and trying a couple of side dishes, including a very peppery carbonara.

After lunch, we went to the da Vinci museum, a small space, hands-on experience, great for kids and for adults who like to play. The museum had working models of some of da Vinci's designs and you could turn cranks and pull levers and play with blocks to your heart's content. So, we did.

Of course, we spent time admiring the Duomo. The construction started in 1296 and was completed in 1436. The dome itself took 16 years to build. The outside is faced with green and pink marble panels, bordered by white and as the Earth moves around the sun, and the clouds scud in and out, the colors seem to change constantly. We didn't take the tour (we didn't go inside a lot of places, trying to limit our exposure to COVID), but we were able to admire the sheer engineering mastery that built a structure that large and beautiful in a time without heavy equipment and modern maths.

The Piazza surrounding the Duomo was busy with tourists but not overcrowded, a benefit of visiting in the off-season. It was lively, but easy to maneuver through the streets and sidewalks. Rome was more a game of dodgems. Romans seemed all in a hurry and very tired of lost tourists slowing them down. The people of Florence were more relaxed. As I said, Florence has a great vibe. For us, we were more about experiencing the people, the out-of-the-way shops, and back streets of a city rather than ticking off a list of tourist spots. We were happy to wander the market place, admire the chalk drawings, and sit with a cup of coffee and people-watch.

Sidewalk Chalk Art near the Duomo, Florence.

Side Trip to Bologna

The train system is the easiest way to explore Italy, short of having a private driver at your beck and call. The train system in Italy, as in most European countries, is fast and convenient and we took advantage of that to visit Bologna for a day, figuring we would look around, have lunch, look around some more. But there were protests going on throughout the country that resulted in a several hours delay of just about every train in Italy, so we got to spend some time in the Florence train depot. We grabbed coffee and croissants, and then people (and doggie) watched. We debated abandoning the trip, decided to stick it out and eventually boarded our train to Bologna.

The Bologna train station is huge. It is a crossroads for Italy and the station has who-knows-how-many levels. We made our way to the street, encountered an orderly protest, and worked our way around it. Bologna is known as a "foodie's paradise" and we climbed a hill to an area crowded with restaurants for every taste and degree of appetite. Unfortunately, we hit at the exact time most were closing for their break between lunch and dinner service. We found a restaurant that was open and had a delightful meal. Of course, I ordered the Bolognese and was not disappointed.

It got dark early; the drizzle didn't help. We headed back towards the train station, taking time to stop at an outdoor Christmas market. We checked out several booths, bought a few trinkets, listened to the music. We may or may not have picked up an abundance of pastries. I am sworn to secrecy.

Overall, Bologna seemed grey and dismal and a little run-down, but I don't think that's a fair assessment. I suspect I need to see it again in sunlight and spend more than a few hours there to get a true feel for the city. And they did have really good pastry.

Let me just say, I LOVE FLORENCE. You know how a place just feels right? That's Florence for me. The people in Florence were more relaxed and friendlier than in Rome. The pace was less hurried but still vibrant. Florence just had a happier vibe going, like it was okay with itself and didn't need to prove anything to anyone. I have marked it down as the number one place in Italy that I want to return to and spend more time, probably at least several weeks. Due to limited time and really, icky weather, we didn't get out to any of the wineries or see much of the countryside. Returning to Florence in warmer weather is definitely on my agenda.

Milan

Milan was on my list of "must-see places before I die" and while I'm not quite ready to die, I will die happier for having seen it. (How's that for a convoluted sentence?)

In hindsight, I realize that somewhere in my mind I had this vision that Milan was going to transform me from someone with no style or taste in clothing to a fashionable, sophisticated

"My GOD, isn't she CONTINENTAL?" type of person. Kind of like the transformation Audrey Hepburn makes in *Sabrina* when she leaves for Paris as a girl and returns as a woman who has grown into herself, so stylish as to be practically unrecognizable.

Alas, I should have gone to Milan as an 18-year-old, or even a 20-something. I am afraid my senior citizen body is no longer suited for sleek Italian dresses and stiletto heels. But oh, I can sure admire the offerings in the shop windows while standing in my comfy running shoes. And yes, we stuck out like the American tourists we were in our running shoes.

Everything about Milan speaks to luxury, from the prices of hotel rooms to dinners out, the jewelry displayed both in stores and on people. The shops carry designer names from Bulgari, Dolce & Gabbana, Armani, Fratelli Rossetti, Gucci, Valentino, Prada—it's a shopaholic's paradise. We were there right before Christmas and the city was decked out in lights. Can excess ever be tasteful? Only in Milan. The Swarovski Christmas tree in the Piazza Duomo was stunning (and sparkly!) and the perfect backdrop for a social media post if you wanted to make all those girls who were mean to you in high school jealous. (Not me, of course. I don't hold a grudge...)

At Christmas, the entire area around the Piazza Duomo is lit up like a magical fairyland. We were visiting in what is typically "off-season" in most places. I don't think the Duomo has an off-season.

The first night we went to the Duomo, the sidewalks were packed with locals and tourists, and while we could have made our way through the shops in the Galleria Vittorio Emanuele, there was no way we wanted to put ourselves into that crushing mass of people during a pandemic. We've seen *Inferno*. Mary Anne and I returned a couple of days later in the afternoon, and were able to actually enjoy the shops, take a selfie in front of the tree, and (most important) grab a gelato.

There were several Christmas markets as well as the normal outdoor markets. There's a huge market in front of Castello Sforzesco with food, souvenirs and gifts, handcrafts, leather goods, clothing... so many little booths that you could spend the day and probably not get to them all. We wound our way through about a quarter of the market and then went into the castle grounds.

As an American, I just can't resist a castle. In Europe, it seems like there's a castle just about everywhere you look. Americans have to go to Disney World and that's not even a real castle. Castello Sforzesco dates back to about 1350, and in 1450, Francesco Sforza started reconstruction and expansion of the castle for his residence. Over the centuries, it has been taken over by both the French and the Spanish, added to, damaged and restored, used as a fort and as the governor's seat. Most of the outer fortifications were destroyed during the Napoleonic rule of Milan. The castle and grounds passed into the possession of the City of Milan after the Unification of Italy in the 19th Century.

Many, if not most, European castles are ruins. Castello Sforzesco is very much intact and it takes little effort to imagine it as it was 500 years ago. It has towers at all four corners, thick walls (in some places, over 20 feet thick), tons of arches, and is rimmed with a parapet of crenellations. (Yeah. That was my new word for the day.) It is the medieval castle that you see in movies, with archers shooting down from the towers and through the narrow slits designed to keep them protected.

We didn't have time to go inside, which I regret, because it contains frescos painted by Leonardo da Vinci and Bramante. The beauty of restoring a castle in Italy in the late 15th century is that you could hire some pretty high-level designers and artists.

We also hit a few charity shops (a favorite hobby) and came away with some treasures. Mary Anne has a much better eye when it comes to fashion (and design and color and everything visual because she's an artist) and she is able to stick her hand into a rack of clothing and pull out pure quality. I have to say, hitting the charity shops in a city known for fashion yields some incredible finds. It also helps if you are a size 8 or smaller. We are convinced that fashionable Milanese women sneak into shops and retag size 2 clothing as size 16 to make us feel bad. That's our story and we're sticking to it.

We found several routes back to our Airbnb which is a nice way of saying we didn't have a clear idea of how to get back but we knew the general direction. This allowed us to discover back streets and a wonderful shop full of antiques and odd items run by an elderly man. The shop was closed but he saw us peering in the windows and opened it up for us. We got to poke around and chat with him. Mary Anne had been looking for a magnifying glass and she was thrilled to find exactly what she had been looking for—a one-of-a-kind antique that was perfect.

For the most part, we didn't have an agenda for every day of our trips. We tended to wander and discover as we go. Some people want to check off all the "must-sees" in each city they visit, making sure they don't miss a thing. We're more relaxed travelers. We hit the grocery stores and the mom-and-pop restaurants and the little family-run stores. For me, the idea is to get a feel for a city, decide what I would like to investigate further on a future trip, or if I want to go back at all. Milan is a place where I will always stick out as an American. The women are far more chic than I ever was or ever will be. I'd love to go back—there's so much more to see—but if I never make it, that's okay, too. It is enough that I could experience Milan at its most magical time.

While we were in Milan, Angie's partner called—her doggo was sick. Now, if you are a dog person, you know exactly how Angie felt. She ended up cutting her trip short to get back to her sweet pup. Mary Anne and I discussed extending our stay in Italy for a few (or more than a few) more days, but the longer I was out of Portugal, the more antsy I became. If we got COVID in Italy, we'd have to quarantine for two weeks. That would be expensive and not fun. I knew even less about the health system in Italy than I did in Portugal. I have private insurance in Portugal; In Italy, we'd both be at the mercy of the over-taxed

Italian health system. If either of us got sick, at least in Portugal I would have some knowledge base to help us.

We decide to stay with our original plan to head back to Portugal and spend a few days in Lisbon. Once there, if anything untoward should happen, I would be on home turf. We could get back to my apartment in three hours by train or by car.

We decided to play it safe. Besides, Mary Anne had never been to Portugal and I had never been to Lisbon. There was no downside to the decision.

Chapter Twenty-Two

Back in Portugal

Honestly, if I needed any confirmation that Portugal is the place for me, it was handed to me on a silver platter. When we left Milan, it was freezing cold and just starting to snow. When our plane touched down in Lisbon, the sun was shining and it was at least 15 (Fahrenheit) degrees warmer. After the grey and rain of Italy, the Portugal sun was just what we needed. I really felt like I was coming home.

Now, that's not to say our Airbnb was warm. Apartments and houses in Portugal are designed to stay cool in the summer and therefore, they stay cool in the winter, too. Just so you know, when an Airbnb in Portugal advertises that it has heat, that most likely means it has space heaters. We put them to good use.

While there wasn't an Irish pub in the neighborhood, there was a bakery directly below us. They had these AMAZING cheese biscuits and the wonderful thing about traveling with Mary Anne is that she believes in enjoying what life drops in your path. When life drops cheese biscuits, you say thank you and nosh away.

Our first full day in Lisbon was spent exploring down towards the waterfront. We (of course) hit Time Out, the HUGE central market and a must visit for foodies and even non-foodies like me. There are dozens of food stalls with every type of food imaginable from traditional Portuguese to all-American burgers and fries. Tons of fresh seafood, Portuguese wines and beers plus places with full bars. Then there are coffee choices and dessert stalls and places to take away cheeses and olives and, in my case, chocolate chip cookies. The stalls are arranged around a huge, chaotic, central eating space. You can hit a variety of stalls and create your own smorgasbord. Seating is sometimes hard to find but people move in and out fairly quickly here.

We did a lot of walking, down to the main plaza, Praça do Comércio, poking about in the shops, reading the historical markers, and basically soaking up the atmosphere. We decided to save the visit up to the castle for the next day. Actually, our feet decided for us. We hit one of the local grocery stores on the way home and picked up some pre-cooked chicken and added a couple of side dishes. There may have been more cheese biscuits.

Castelo de São Jorge

While we had no set itinerary for Lisbon, our mode of wandering and moving in the approximate direction of where we wanted to go had given us enough of the basic layout of Lisbon that it was easy to decide where we would go on our second full day.

On my trip to Europe with my mom, I learned the phrase "ABC Tour." ABC stands for Another Bloody Castle. While the tour guides might get sick of castles, it's going to be a long time before I start taking them for granted. Many castles are reduced to ruins and you have to kind of imagine how they looked in their prime. Not so the castle of Saint George that stands guard over Lisbon. There is no way you could look up at that castle on the hill and *NOT* want to go.

We were very wise and took an Uber as far as we could up the hill that the castle sits atop. Even then, traffic was backed up and we ended up hiking about ten minutes (or maybe it was five and seemed like ten) up the steep hill to the castle grounds. There are a bunch of shops at the entrance (of course), all doing a brisk business. Mary Anne and I fell in love with one particular shop that had gorgeous pottery and dishes, plus the traditional tiles. When and if I get a permanent place that does not come furnished, I am going back there to outfit my kitchen.

We paid a nominal entrance fee and were admitted onto the grounds. The view was nothing short of amazing. We were drawn to the edge of the grounds to take advantage of the panoramic view, looking out over the entire city of Lisbon, the water, the 25 de Abril Bridge (the longest suspension bridge in Europe) all the way across to the Cristo Rei statue, which was inspired by the Christ the Redeemer statue in Rio.

We took a brief coffee break before heading into the castle area. The castle was built in the 11th century by the Moors who occupied the Iberian Peninsula. (Many of the names of cities and towns in Portugal are actually Moorish.) It was built as a military stronghold: The panoramic views we were enjoying helped ensure that no enemy could launch a surprise attack.

King Alfonso Henriquez, along with an army of crusaders, captured the fort from the Moors in the 12th century, and it served as a royal residence up until the 1765 earthquake. As with most centuries-old buildings, it underwent changes and additions. It's now a blend of Moorish and medieval architecture with 11 towers, horseshoe arches, yep, my new word: crenellations.

The castelo is named for Saint George, the patron saint of England which would seem strange—until you discover that King João presented the castle as a wedding gift to his English wife, Philippa of Lancaster in 1387. I'd say he set a pretty high bar in the gift-giving competition.

We strolled the courtyard of the castle, enjoying the gardens, reading the various informative plaques, looking at just about everything: stones, the way trees were rooted, the angles of the arches. There's a flock of peacocks that wander through the grounds. We got some close up looks at them and yes, of course we were delighted each and every time one displayed its plumage. There are some things in life that make you realize how amazing and unique our experience here is—things you never get tired of seeing and you never stop being gobsmacked by (as Mary Anne would say). Peacocks are one of those things for me. The colors are just brilliant, deep and iridescent.

We climbed up stone steps to walk the battlements. While the views from the grounds had been gorgeous, the extra height allowed us to see for miles around. We were lucky to have such a clear day: Lisbon laid out in all directions was spectacular. Well worth the climb and I'm not going to lie: It's (as we say in Boston) wicked awesome to walk the battlements of a medieval castle. You can feel the history of the place and imagine what it might have been like to be a soldier on patrol—in a totally romanticized way of course: not thinking about the cold, the fact that people hadn't bathed in ages, and you know, the possibility of someone trying to kill you.

Our feet were complaining and our stomachs were growling. We walked back down the hill in the approximate direction of the waterfront and Praça do Comércio. The various restaurants lining the plaza were doing a brisk business. We found a table and gratefully put our packages down. Our feet recovered while we ate our lunch, basking in the mid-afternoon sun.

We trudged back to our Airbnb, with a stop for groceries and a check-in at the bakery to see if, by any lucky chance, there might be some cheese biscuits left. There were.

Neither one of us is a big night activity person. Pretty much, once we're in, we're in for the night. We settled in with our laptops and spent some time catching up on our work. After such a big lunch, we were happy with a light supper. The Airbnb had a well-appointed kitchen. Mary Anne made a delicious chicken soup that we paired with fresh Portuguese bread, slathered with butter. A perfect ending to a full day.

All our activities so far had involved walking down towards the waterfront. On our last full day in Lisbon, we decided to walk up and explore some of the neighborhoods. We found an area with antique and second-hand shops, discovering items that we would love to have—if we lived in Lisbon. That's part of the fun and one of the frustrations of traveling: You see things that would be just perfect if you lived in that place. You check out real estate prices and neighborhoods and kind of plan out in your head the way you'd furnish your place. At least I do. So, when I see a perfect antique desk at a great price, I start planning a life based around the desk. Or sofa. Or armoire. All imagination, of course, but that's the way my brain works. I think a lot of people like to put themselves into these imaginary scenarios. There's a reason why *The Secret Life of Walter Mitty* (or, for the Brits, *Reggie Perrin*) was so popular: Traveling shows you new things and it triggers your imagination. It starts that "What if" question in your head. What if I did live here? Which leads to the How question: How could I do that?

You may or may not decide to actually move and you may discover new things about a place that makes it easier to pass on the idea, but I think anything that gets you thinking about possibilities is good for your soul. That's what travel is all about: expanding your understanding of other places and cultures and opening up your mind to new ideas, ways of doing things, and most of all, possibilities.

Chapter Twenty-Three

Sugar Comas and Harry Potter

We took the train from Lisbon to Faro and met with our hired driver to carry us back to Santa Luzia. I was excited to show my apartment to Mary Anne. We got her settled in and took a break. There would be plenty of time to show her the village and Tavira and any other place we wanted to go. But after ten days of traveling for me and 20 days for her, it was good to unpack our bags (and start the laundry) without an eye towards repacking them.

Mary Anne settled into her room in my apartment and we fell into our pattern from when we shared a place in Florida. She is a much better cook than I am, but I could at least keep us in fresh croissants and pastéis de nata from the bakery below.

We both worked, of course, But the five-hour time difference between Portugal and the East Coast gave us opportunities to explore the village and Tavira. We hit the markets and charity shops as well as the Saturday flea market where Mary Anne picked up found objects perfect for her artwork. The dining room table became her workbench while I happily lounged on the sofa with my laptop. The days developed the steady rhythm of work and play and just quiet normality.

Ah, but Christmas was coming. I am not at all religious so I take great delight in celebrating EVERY holiday in December. We made sure we had everything we needed to continue our now annual three-day tradition of cupcakes, pastries, and a *Harry Potter* marathon. I won't say that all work stopped, but the vast majority of our time was spent drinking wine, watching *Harry Potter*, and eating ourselves into a sugar coma. If you can't be a kid at Christmas, when can you?

New Year's Eve came and went. I did NOT subject Mary Anne to my usual New Year's tradition of watching *Kill Bill I and 2*. I'm probably a better person for it.

Even in the Rain

We had one more trip planned before Mary Anne had to go home. If you ask a Portuguese person what their favorite city is, a striking majority will say Porto. We flew up to Porto for a couple of days to explore the city.

Frankly, January is not the best month to visit Porto. It's relatively cold (40s and 50s F) and it's the height of the rainy season. (An expat friend in Porto assures me that rainy season is year-round there.) We landed in Porto on a typically overcast, drizzly afternoon and checked into our hotel.

Now, if you're used to US hotels, European hotels (not all, let's say some) have a different aesthetic. If you're staying at a large chain, then yes, you'll get that fairly typical room with two queen beds. But in some places, particularly if the hotel is older or in a more rural area, many times you have the choice between two twin beds and one queen. We were staying at a budget hotel that was fairly new. We walked into our room and it was... small. Incredibly clean and bright. The twin beds were pushed together so they looked like a double bed, but were made up separately. Okay. A little strange, but the price was right and the hotel was clean and well-located. Even pushed together, the beds took up about 85% of the main room. The bathroom was tight, but again, clean and well lit. There was a small space to hang our things and fortunately we were traveling light. I've spent more money in "boutique" hotels whose rooms were just as small and had fewer amenities. The room had everything we needed. It would do just fine. We dropped our things and bundled up to explore.

The hotel was located in the historic center of Porto, right across from the Igreja de Santo Ildefonso. There is a small plaza in front of the church that had a few vendors and an open-air COVID testing site. We walked up the street (those hills in

Albufeira taught me that much), looking for a place to have dinner later, checking the shops, and generally getting our bearings for tomorrow's activities. We passed a restaurant that, after perusing the posted menu, looked promising. Actually, looked delicious. Many restaurants close between lunch and dinner, so we noted the time they'd reopen and made plans to return.

We tend to work a grid, or at least keep track of our general direction. We crossed over one block from the street the hotel was on and started back down the next parallel street. We found the Pingo Doce grocery store and knew if worse came to worse, we could always get snacky snacks. The Christmas lights were still up and as we walked, they came on, ribbons of light that arched over the streets, creating a surreal cityscape in the misty gloom. We came back to the church and took a right, finding a street thriving with shops and restaurants. Including a gelato shop. We watched the server behind the counter scoop gelato into waffle cones, packing and layering the gelato so it looked like a flower. Mary Anne's eyes met mine. Didn't matter how cold and rainy it was—we were coming back here after dinner.

Rain is a given in Porto but I was unprepared for the cold. I was spoiled by the milder temperatures in the Algarve. I had, once again, not brought a warm enough coat with me. We went back to the hotel to warm up and check emails, spending enough time that we wouldn't be the first ones at the door when the restaurant reopened.

The restaurant proved to be better than we had hoped. Like the hotel, it was fairly new and a little trendy. For the life of me, I can't remember what we had, but it was good enough that we decided to go back for our special "last night in Porto" dinner. We walked the short way back down to the church, which had become our navigational touchstone. We took the right-hand jog onto the main street and made our way back to the gelato shop. Even in the relative cold, the gelato hit the spot. We wandered back to the hotel, happy and sated.

The next day we found a place for a full breakfast in a small hotel near the church. It was one of those older hotels, oozing old world charm, and the dining room had the look of a ballroom that had been converted to a dining area. Lots of dark antiques, velvet upholstery, linen table cloths, quiet, unhurried service. The perfect start to any day.

This day was dedicated to our main modus operandi: nothing planned besides hitting some charity shops and leaving the day open to discovery. I found a warm coat in one of the shops for €15 and wore it out the door. The day was overcast with patches of sun, and when you're walking up and down hills, you stay warm enough. We did a full exploration of what was, for us, "the main drag," working our way to a park and then working our way back. We walked into any store that caught our eye, stopped to admire churches and buildings in general, tile work and doorways. We may have stopped for a gelato on the way back...

Basically, we got our bearings for the next day, which was our full-on tourist day. Mary Anne had bought tickets to Livraria Lello, one of the most beautiful bookshops in the world. The ticket allows you to skip the line, and, if you buy something, it acts like a coupon—the price is deducted from your purchase. It's a sure bet that if we walk into a bookstore, we are going to walk out with a purchase. Buying entry tickets was a no-brainer.

We started walking Rua de Santa Caterina, using our "moving in the approximate direction of where we think we want to end up" method of navigating. While this generally works, we quickly figured out that we were not quite where we wanted to be. We checked in at a tourist center near a busy intersection, right across from one of the most famous churches in Porto: The Chapel of Santa Caterina. It is amazingly beautiful, covered in blue azulejo tile. No wonder this corner was so busy. Groundbreaking on the chapel was in the late 18th century, but the exterior tiles weren't added until 1929. I am a big fan of anything blue and white and the chapel put me on overwhelm. The tiles represent the lives (really deaths and martyrdom, because Catholics) of Saint Catherine (who apparently has her own cult—you go girl!) and St. Francis of Assisi. I'm very sure you could spend days looking at all the tiles and not find all the nuances to the stories they tell. It's one of many "blue-tile" churches in Porto and while it's not the largest (that honor may go to the Porto Cathedral but don't quote me on it), it is certainly, for me, the most striking. It's got a wow-factor for sure.

The Chapel of Santa Caterina, Porto

With confirmation that we had been heading in the right direction, we continued on and made a little detour due to construction in the area. We popped up a level to another shopping district and made our way to Livraria Lello. In spite of the steady drizzle, there was a long line of people waiting their turn to get into the shop. We went to the front and presented our tickets and were inside and dry in a minute or two.

If you love books, Livraria Lello is something out of a fairy tale. For a bookaholic like me, this is the place you want to be when you die. I walked around thinking, "I want this in my house. I want a library just like this."

Livraria Lello (yeah, I know, it's a tongue twister; welcome to Portuguese) is one of the oldest bookshops in Portugal and rated one of the top bookstores in the world. It was founded in 1869 by Ernesto Chardron and in 1881, after his death, it was bought by José Lello who was shortly joined in the partnership by his brother António. The brothers bought out other bookstores and in 1906, they opened the shop where it now stands.

The shop has two floors, joined by the most amazing staircases that yes, perhaps, possibly, were the inspiration for the shifting staircases at Hogwarts. Both floors are lined front to back with books and we found the English language books easily. As you come through the entrance, you see the main staircase in the center of the store, branching off to a suspended staircase that leads to the upper galleries on either side. The ceiling is a huge, stain glass skylight designed by the Dutch master Samuel Van Krieken. I made it to the back area of the upper floor, a room dedicated to José Saramago, the only Portuguese language writer to be awarded the Nobel Prize in Literature.

The second floor of Livraria Lello.

Not all the rooms and collections are open to the public. The shop itself is not large in the time of super-stores, but every inch is beautiful. The ceiling and interiors are actually painted plaster, designed to look like carved wood. The staircases are gently curved and the circular motif is carried out in the plaster detail in the ceilings. The shop was crowded, in spite of the limitations on the number of people allowed in due to COVID. I suspect many of the people just wanted to see the "Harry Potter bookstore" and weren't really there for the books. And that's okay because the shop itself is something anyone can appreciate.

We left with our purchases and went back to the area of shops, finding a papelaria, something neither of us can resist. We crossed back down through the construction zone and started working our way back to the hotel. Our feet and legs were tuckered out and neither one of us has a problem with saying we need a break.

The next day, we visited the "hidden house of Porto." The house is three feet wide, sandwiched between two churches, Carmo and Carmelitas. (Yes, more blue tiles! I was delighted.) I was particularly curious about visiting *Igreja dos Carmelitas Descalços* which was built for Carmelite nuns. We've had a running joke in our family about the Carmelites. My aunt was a Sister of St. Joseph. (Think yards of black drapery and the full nun hood thing, but no wings.) My sister and I went to visit her at the Convent one time and my sister rolled out the idea that maybe she should become a nun. Without hesitating, my aunt said, "Try the Carmelites—they'll take anybody." (Nun-snark. It's a thing.) We all knew my sister was NOT nun material. I'm pretty sure even the Carmelites would have passed. Very much a good thing for all parties.

But I was curious about Carmelites. The church was built in the 17th century (the Carmelite monks had to wait for their church until the next century). If you look at the façade, it's easy to think it's all one big church. Look again and you can see this narrow space that separates them. It's a house. For very thin people. For real—it was inhabited up through the 1980s.

We toured the church first. I did not tell the Carmelite nun joke to any of the people there. The church, of course, is gorgeous, even in dim light. Old, polished wood pews, a ton of gold—gilded, baroque style carvings, and a gorgeous domed ceiling. We toured up and around and at one point were in an area where you could look down and see human bones. Did I dream that? Nope. Human bones. Okay then. Moving on...

We crossed into the skinniest house in Porto, a place that can only be toured by walking sideways. Fun Fact: It's classified as the narrowest house in Porto and—get this—*one* of the narrowest houses in Portugal. WHAT? There's more?

Most people seemed to get claustrophobic pretty quickly—you didn't tour the house so much as poke your head in a few spots, then squeeze by someone else to get out. From there, we could go to the Carmo side—the church for the Carmelite monks. The center aisle of the church is a series of arches leading to an altar that has enough gilding to finance a small country. Very beautiful and it would be over the top, except this is the way they did things back then. It beats the hell out of 1970s harvest gold and avocado green.

We found a restaurant with outdoor seating across the way in a park like area. The weather wasn't super-conducive to eating outside, but both of us felt more comfortable in the open air. We had a chance to get a good look at the Douro River. We had considered taking a boat tour of the river but decided it was just a tad too cold for that.

We fully intended to go back to the restaurant we found on our first night, but it was closed when we got there. We walked up the street, but none of the other eateries appealed. I joked that we could eat in the Pingo Doce Restaurant. We made our way over to it, thinking maybe we'd just get some food and eat in the room. But then Mary Anne spied a restaurant menu on a nearby building. The menu looked good and we went in.

Any possibility of a table?

Could we be finished by 9:00 pm when they had a large party coming in?

It was only around 7:30. No problem.

The hostess brought us through the restaurant into a back area that was a glassed-in grotto. Candlelight, linen tablecloths. She brought us a complimentary house sangria, made with mangos and magic. Yes, of course we ordered a big pitcher. I think we both ordered steak and it arrived perfectly cooked, tender and flavorful. None of the service was rushed and we still had time for coffee. It was the perfect last night in town meal.

Did we go for gelato after? I honestly can't remember, but I wouldn't bet against it.

Flying back to the Algarve the next day was a quick reminder of why I chose to live in the south. The sun was shining and the temperature was about 15 degrees warmer. The sun makes all the difference here. It sounds superficial, but you have to really like rain and overcast skies to live in Porto. Some people do.

Honestly, the vibe in Porto is so good, it overcomes a lot of the downsides of the climate. But I need the sun. Lots of it. Another trip to Porto is on the list, but it will be in warmer weather.

Chapter Twenty-Four

One Year In

A week later, it was time for Mary Anne to go back to the States. The first few days after she left felt a lot lonelier. We had fallen back into our housemates' pattern and there was a lot of comfort in that. She has a standing invitation to return anytime.

As my first anniversary of living in Portugal arrived, I took the time to look back to see how far I had come.

I was officially a resident, with an ID card and everything. I had a real apartment, a permanent place to call home base. I have worked 'round to feeling like the landlord's furnishings are "my" furnishings. I have added things as I go, mostly things for the kitchen (which came equipped with three French presses but no garlic press). I bought a mattress topper for Mary Anne. I had been sleeping on a rock-hard bed for months. It didn't occur to me that I didn't have to. Once she left, that mattress topper migrated over to my bedroom. I'll get one for the guest room when the time comes.

The bed is just one example of how little I do to put my imprint on a place. I have one picture hanging up. I am unsure about putting more holes in the wall, even though I am a rock star at spackling. While I am more comfortable in this apartment than when I first arrived, I still haven't made it "home." For now, it is enough that it no longer feels strange to me. It is definitely my place. With the exception of the garbage trucks that come by after midnight, I no longer hear all the night noises: people walking home late from the bars, fishermen leaving later than usual, the occasional car or truck. I feel safe here. I still feel like the stranger in town, the Americana, but I don't feel any malice or put out by it. I have not yet integrated into the community and probably won't until my language skills are better.

I think a lot of people would find this lonely. There's a reason why expats tend to find each other and become friends: it's not just the commonalities of language and background; it's the unspoken truth that you're all outsiders trying to fit in. Maybe I'll always be an outsider. But every time someone wishes me *bom dia* or gives me an encouraging smile, I feel a little less outside. This is my home and eventually I will know the people and they will know me. I will take my small victories in the nods and greetings that don't go any deeper, yet. It's on me to learn the language and be interested in people, not the other way around.

In a consultation the other day, the woman I was speaking with asked me what my biggest surprise was in moving here. I had to think about it because it wasn't a surprise when it was happening—It was more of a realization, one that I didn't reach for well over a year.

I wasn't at all prepared for the level of anxiety that was with me constantly. It's not a fear for my safety—I feel much safer here than I did in Florida. It was the anxiety of "not knowing" and that is still with me somewhat. The difference is that now I recognize I have it.

Face it: In 2020 and 2021, the entire world was in the middle of the pandemic and people's anxiety levels were understandably maxed. So, moving to another country? It took me a while to figure out that I had pretty much doubled that COVID anxiety. I mean, really, when you're already freaked out, what's one more thing to freak out about? But anxiety is cumulative and there were many times when my head was swimming or I had brain fog or it was just all too much.

Many people, too many people, in 2025 are experiencing that same level of anxiety. The US government is purposely unstable, institutions are being destroyed, orders and policies are being sent out and then rescinded or struck down by the courts. No one has any idea what will happen tomorrow. The question of should I stick it out or should I move somewhere—anywhere—else is on people's minds.

That's a decision only you can make for yourself. Everyone's circumstances are different. Everyone's resources and ability to adapt are different. I hope this book has shone the light on various aspects of moving overseas that you don't hear about in the guidebooks and the glossy magazines.

Most of this first year was spent figuring out the mechanics of things. The most important was getting my residency appointment completed and becoming an official resident of Portugal. I had more anxiety about this than was warranted. Yes, it was important to get done. But SEF (now AIMA) had extended temporary residency visas due to COVID and continued to do so because of the backlog. Not having my permanent residence card was only an issue if I wanted to travel in and out of Portugal multiple times. With COVID lockdowns, most people weren't traveling. So, it was a non-issue for me. Four years later, they are still extending visas and trying to catch up on backlogs as they transition more of the immigration process to online systems.

It was definitely well-founded anxiety for people who needed to travel back to the States for whatever reason. You can only go in and out twice on the temporary residency visa, and with appointments being pushed back multiple times, people who had to travel were afraid they wouldn't be able to get back in. My appointment was pushed back five months. As restrictions lifted, the backlog was eased and postponements were for shorter periods of time. Did it affect some people? Definitely. Did I need to stress about it as much as I did? No. But I didn't know that *while* I was stressing.

And that was just one thing in a continuous chain of things that I needed to take care of or learn how to navigate. Grocery shopping is no longer stressful for me. The check-out process is much less stressful now that I know people aren't going to critique how quickly I bag my groceries. There is still a little stress: the number of people in the store, the smell of fish, not being able to find things or remember which store I had found something in. I still don't know what the hell I am looking at sometimes. But I do have my go-to stores and I have learned my way around the aisles. It's a huge improvement from the early days when the grocery aisles were a blur of colors.

Some People Leave

There are times I think "Whatever possessed me?" but those times are few and far between. I don't think anyone ever makes a huge life change without wondering if it was a mistake. About half the Americans who move to Portugal end up leaving again in two to five years. (FYI: Those time frames coincide with long-term residency visa times.)

People leave Portugal for as many reasons as they come to Portugal. Portugal has an entirely different culture and when you've been born and raised in the hustle and grind culture of the US, the slower pace and different priorities take getting used to. Most Americans are used to instant gratification and conveniences. Heck, before I left, I was using Door Dash to deliver pastries to my house. How lazy is that? (And yeah, there's a reason I live next to a bakery.)

It's an adjustment and some people never adjust. They miss certain conveniences like dishwashers, clothes dryers, or a wide variety of prepped food at the grocery stores. Can you get these things? Yes, but that's going to come at a price. For the people who moved here, sold on the fable that living in Portugal is cheap and easy, they're not going to be happy.

Portugal has a lower cost of living, especially compared to the larger US cities, but it is no longer a low-cost country. Home prices and rents have gone up drastically in the past few years; Lisbon is now one of the more expensive European cities to live in.

The days of finding a two-bedroom apartment in a small city for €500 or €600 are gone. Yes, if you go to a rural area, you can find that. But you'll need a car and a good grasp of Portuguese. Certain glossy magazines are still touting the idea that you can stop at a charming restaurant and get a three-course lunch with wine for €7.00. If you find that place, let me know.

The hardest thing about Portugal and the biggest reason why expats leave is the most obvious: *It's a foreign country.*

You are always the other. If you don't speak the language, you feel left out. While many Portuguese speak some English (most of the younger people are quite fluent), the conversations you overhear are in Portuguese. Your sense of self, your place in the world gets rattled. In the States, you fit in, you were at a certain level in the pecking order, you could navigate your world with confidence. You miss your family and friends but more than that, you miss being in a place where you knew you belonged.

Many people never get comfortable in their new country. I am still not completely comfortable and may never be. But I'm comfortable enough for me.

Leaving Is Not Always a Choice.

I met one couple (he British, she US) who were absolutely thrilled to be in Portugal. They were together, happy, looking to buy a permanent place. About six months after arriving, he had a massive heart attack. They got a masterclass in how the health system works in Portugal. They had private insurance and he received great care. He recovered and they continued with their lives. They contracted for a nice apartment in town, and a week before they were to close on it, he had a massive stroke. Again, between public and private sectors, he received great care, but this time, his health was not recovered. She was here, basically alone, with a very ill husband. She confided to me that she had never made any major decisions in their marriage—it was always a joint decision and she often followed his lead, first, because he was very smart, and second because they usually felt the same way about things. But she had spent decades not really doing anything on her own: They were a team. Once he was healthy enough to travel, they returned to the States, close to her family so she could have the support system she needed.

It's not that Portugal wasn't a good fit for them. They would have been happy living here for as long as they could. It's that they could not physically stay here—she needed help that only her family could give.

The Hardest Part About Being an Expat (for Me)

Some days the Earth's gravitational field is noticeably stronger. The air is heavy. The clouds are heavy. The world is lethargic and dim and muffled. There is not enough coffee.

The downside of moving to a new country is that you can't physically be with friends and family when they need you. You can't hug over Zoom. You can't sit side by side in comfortable silence or clink glasses to toast a life well lived. You can't squeeze a hand to let them know that they are inside your heart.

People ask me if I get lonely. I seldom do. I don't have the lonely gene. I have many friends and acquaintances, plenty of family members who I love and like, but being alone is restful for me. I have always been able to entertain myself.

But some days and weeks are hard. The week my longtime friend lost her mother and I couldn't be there for her. I discovered another friend was having some memory issues. I suspected it was exacerbated by the isolation of lockdown. A third friend had a looming housing crisis. Several have had major health issues.

I can't fix any of these things, whether I am there or here. But if I lived closer, I could offer support in some physical form perhaps. Holding hands, bringing a meal. Fetching groceries.

But I'm 4,000 miles away.

The hardest part of being an expat for me is not being with family and friends, in hard times and good times. Yes, you make new friends, some of whom will become good friends. But there's no history. The bonds haven't yet been formed, much less strengthened. It's not the same. Yet.

Time does not equal quality of relationship. Is a twenty-year relationship worth saving if 17 of those years have been bad? (No.) Do I have a friend of four years who I am as close to as friends of 40 years? (Yes.)

Time and quality of relationships make our lives. People make our lives. And being there, for the people you love, is one of the most important things you will ever do.

Distance makes it hard. But not impossible.

Technology has made it easier to "be there." I schedule Zoom calls to chat. I can send surprise cupcakes or have a pizza delivered. I can order groceries (or booze!) and have them delivered. I am awake when all their nearby friends are asleep. They can call and I will answer.

I am more mindful of keeping tabs on my people. In the States, I was lazy about relationships because it was easy to get to my friends. Many were within a 100-mile radius or a two-hour plane ride. If someone needed me, I could get to them quickly.

I have friends who can't fly over here due to health reasons or personal responsibilities. It's frustrating. I can't physically be there. They can't physically be here. But it's part of the deal. When I lived in Hawaii, it was seven time zones and a minimum of ten hours of flight time to get back to my family. I am actually closer now.

A Year of Unknowns

There were things I knew and expected going in, like I would need to buy private health insurance, but it would be much cheaper than in the US. There were things I knew that I didn't know, like how I was going to set up my taxes. And then, of course, there were many, many things I did not know that I did not know. Those created some interesting moments of panic—I mean fun. And now I am very sure that there are many more things that I have yet to uncover.

My first year in Portugal was a year of the unknown. A year when I hit overwhelm on a regular basis. But also, a year when I realized that I could handle anything thrown at me. I learned to take things one at a time, mostly because there were many days when I could only handle one thing. But I also learned that I didn't have to do everything all at once. Everything got done within the needed time frames if I broke down the steps and tasks.

I also learned to slow down. Nothing happens fast in Portugal and, while it took some adjusting, I really love the pace. Not because I am older, but because I am calmer.

Every country has a culture, and for the US, that culture is movement, constant movement. It's a fast pace and everyone claims to be busy, even if they're not. We have to look busy; we have to be busy. We have to be doing something to prove that we are not slackers, that we are go-getters.

One of my favorite quotes is from journalist George Monbiot: *"If wealth was the inevitable result of hard work and enterprise, every woman in Africa would be a millionaire."*

Once I stepped away from the US, I realized that the hustle and grind, working 24/7/365 culture was a false construct. Americans are sold on the idea that we just have to work hard and we will be millionaires. We believe that if we work harder, faster, longer that we will finally break through whatever financial ceiling we've been laboring under and finally "make it."

I suppose if I lived in Lisbon or even Porto, I might feel and see a bit more of the hustle culture. Make no mistake: the Portuguese people work very hard, often for not much money. But they also are very clear on what their priorities are: family, helping each other, Christiano Ronaldo...

There is a balance to life here that you don't see in the States. People take the time to talk. It still stuns me that if I ask a Portuguese person "How are you?" they actually tell me—the good and the bad. "How are you" is a real question here. In the States, no one wants to admit that they are struggling or not being efficient or are worried about paying the bills. Here, what you see is what you get.

People ask if there is anything I would do differently in moving to Portugal.

The answer is yes.

I would have done it sooner.

Afterword: You Don't Have to be Brave to Move Abroad

Here's what you DO have to be...

You don't have to be brave to move abroad. (Okay, maybe a little.) There are other traits that you need much more than courage if you're going to make the leap to living overseas. As it turns out, the better you are at these, the less courage you need because you'll feel like you know what you are doing. You won't, but you'll feel better about it. Kidding! Sort of.

So, what do you need to be?

Be Organized

Paperwork: Moving to a new country takes a lot of organizing. The paperwork of applying for a residency visa seems overwhelming while you are doing it, and when it's done, you'll wonder why you thought it was so hard. It's because it's a new process for you and every step is unknown. While I had a checklist for my Portuguese D7 visa, there were items I had to figure out. For example, I needed to send in a "Certified Copy" of my passport. What the heck is a certified copy? How do I get it certified? It turns out that I just needed to make a color copy of my passport (the picture page), and have a notary stamp it. (For the record, Amscot and bank notaries can only stamp certain types of documents. Find a regular notary.) It was simple... once I figured out what they were asking for. The expat groups on Facebook have lots of advice on every step of the process.

I forgot to bring a copy of my birth certificate with me. I had my passport and driver's license and I just wasn't thinking that far back into my past. I haven't needed it so far, but it later occurred to me that maybe I should have a copy. Having digitized copies of most documents will probably get you through—you don't need to carry paper files of everything in your life. (Having things like five years of tax returns on a back-up drive would be handy. Just sayin.)

Meds: You need to think ahead about what you will need. Get copies of all your prescriptions from your doctors to give to your new doctors. Get your medical records. Try to get 90 days of any medications you will need. The first few months are a blur of setting yourself up, getting insurance, figuring out where to buy groceries, learning your way around. You don't want to be stressing about getting an important prescription refilled before you have figured out who your new doctor is.

Clothing: I lived in Florida for 30 years. Portugal gets a bit chilly, especially at night. I didn't have a warm coat or a lot of sweaters. I brought my fleece and some sweats, knowing I would buy more once I was here. I didn't need to bring three coats, five sweaters, two sets of sweats, and every pair of socks I owned. I do wish I had brought more than one pair of fuzzy socks. That oversight has been rectified. Portugal has fuzzy socks, too.

I thought that everyone in Europe would be much better dressed than me. (Well, actually, most people are better dressed than I am.) I didn't bring a lot of clothes because I figured I would need to buy clothes there to level up and blend in. If you're moving to Paris or Milan, you will need to level up. I live in a fishing village. We all walk around in jeans and athleisure wear and nobody is trying to impress anyone. The ladies, as ladies do everywhere, dress better than the men. Some wear heels. Most of us are in running shoes. Most of the sidewalks and many of the streets are cobblestone. Walking in heels on those stones spells sure death for me. I will leave high heels to the more nimble.

Do Your Research. People moving to a new country ask a lot of questions that can be answered by a simple Google search.

What's the weather like in February? (Google it.) How much is it to rent a two-bedroom apartment in Lagos? (Google it.) Can you drink the water? (Don't get me started.) We live in an age where information is at our fingertips. Misinformation is also at our fingertips. Learning how to research involves knowing how to evaluate the source of that information. Anyone can put a video on YouTube and make all sorts of claims. You might prefer to get your information from peer reviewed studies or sites that have credibility.

And yes, a quick plug: I offer "Ask Me Anything" chats via my SubStack site. You can book a one-hour Zoom call with me to talk about your specific situation. Learn more about it here: https://barbaragrassey.substack.com/p/lets-talk

Organize your money. Money solves a lot of problems. Forgot something? Buy it here. Your new apartment doesn't have heat? (Welcome to Portugal.) Buy a couple of space heaters. Whatever you have budgeted for your initial expenses, set aside a little more. A lot of people move to a new country and have just the bare minimum necessary to get their visa approved. You don't want to be in that situation. If the country requires that you have income of $1,000 a month and $8,000 in savings, then increase those numbers by 20% or more. You don't want to be scraping to pay bills or afraid you're going to get kicked out of the country if you can't show the necessary reserves. When it comes to money, more is better. No matter where you live.

Set up online/automatic payments for your ongoing bills. I've been paying my bills online for years. I set up all my recurring business expenses to go to one credit card and each month I pay it off. My few stateside personal bills are automatically debited from my Florida account. I learned how to transfer money via Wise once I was here and had my bank account set up. You now need to have your bank account set up before your visa is approved. It's a pain in the neck to do from the States but it can be done. If you're taking a scouting trip to your new country, try to set it up when you're in country. Check to see what you will need to have in place *before* you leave the US for your trip. It can take a few days to a few weeks to get your Portuguese NIF (individual tax ID number) which you will need to open a bank account. It's easy to do that from the States using an online service like NIFOnline or Bordr. Opening a bank account long distance is not nearly as easy.

Have a plan going in. Set up where you are going to live, whether you buy a house, rent, or use short term rentals like Airbnbs. If you're not sure where you want to live permanently, choose an area that will be easy for you when you first get there. I chose the Algarve because it was touristy which meant that many people spoke some English. I did ***not*** go to a small village in the middle of the country that lacked the amenities I would need, like a grocery store and restaurants within walking distance, and where only a few people spoke English. If you've never lived "off grid" and that is your goal, you might want to get the lay of the land and live ***on*** the grid before you make that second jump. Will you need a car? Getting a car is another learning curve that involves registration, insurance, inspections.

How long is your US driver's license valid after you officially become a resident? How do you get a Portuguese (or whatever country) license? Try to keep your plan as simple as possible, at least for the first six, maybe 12 months. You need time to acclimate. Some of the things you thought you wanted might change. Have a plan that makes allowances for that. Flexibility is key.

Be Willing to Leave "Things" Behind

One of the hardest things for people to do is to pare down their belongings. Many possessions represent events and times in our lives that are important to us. But some things don't. We accumulate a lot of stuff with each passing year. Keep the stuff with true sentimental value. Get rid of anything that you can easily replace. (Yes, I'm thinking of all that Pyrex that I somehow thought I needed to keep.)

I came to Portugal with one big suitcase, one carry-on suitcase, my computer case and, because my flight had been delayed by a week, a Nantucket bag with the necessities I had picked up that week.

I was shocked when I saw all the Facebook photos of expats arriving at various airports with multiple suitcases—sometimes as many as 20. It turns out it is much cheaper to pay for extra bags than it is to ship stuff. I was miffed that I had to pay extra because my big suitcase was overweight. Now I would recommend that you keep your suitcase within the weight limits and pay for an extra bag. You can bring more stuff for the same price.

There are "things" you can bring, but they make no sense to bring them. First of all, the electrical grid is different and the plugs are different. The only thing I have that runs on a US-style plug is my laptop. That gets plugged into an adapter. (A friend gave me two of those and they have been lifesavers.)

You will wear different style clothing here. You can buy hairdryers and kitchen appliances and linens, fabulous dishes and Italian cutlery. It's a new life. For about the same price as shipping everything, you can buy new.

I donated as much of my stuff as I could bear and managed to get everything I own into a small, five foot by five foot, air conditioned storage unit. I didn't have any furniture to store. If you are not sure that living the expat life will be for you, I recommend storing your stuff. If you own a house and feel comfortable renting it out for a year or two while you make sure you will make the full transition, do that.

I moved with the knowledge that if worse came to worse and I didn't like it here, I could move back. I have also learned the cheapest way to ship things over here when I am ready. But a year later, I don't *want* to bring *all that stuff* here. I don't miss most of it. I like not having a lot of belongings to worry about. It's very freeing to have room in your closets and drawers. Also, the less stuff you have, the easier it is to organize.

Be Open to New Ways of Doing Things

When I lived in Florida, we had a lot of transplants and "snowbirds"—retirees who spent their winter months in sunny Florida and went back up north for the rest of the year. We got very used to hearing "That's not how we do it back in [insert any northern state]" to which we would roll our eyes and mutter, "Yeah. Well, you're in Florida now, Bucko." Okay. I was probably the only who added Bucko.

Different places do things differently. That's kind of the deal. If you want everything to be the same as it was "back home" then stay back home. Be happy.

I have had to relearn all sorts of stuff. I was already familiar with packing my own groceries thanks to Aldi. I don't leave the house without a couple of reusable shopping bags now. I automatically look for the little ticket machine in banks, post offices, doctors' offices, etc. (Think of the little ticket machines at the deli counter but these have a touchscreen with options.) I still don't know what most of the options are. I click on the option that looks about right, wait until my number is called and then find out if I guessed right or not. Sometimes I have to go back, take a new number, and start again. Eventually I will be able to choose the right ticket type, just as I am now able to navigate the ATM in Portuguese.

Some of the "new ways" are just different versions of the old ways. People complain about government bureaucracy and how slowly things get done here. Have you ever dealt with the SBA? Or the IRS? DMV? Nothing moves fast in government; I don't care what country you're in. (Though I will say the US Embassy in Lisbon is on top of stuff—just my experience.)

People (Americans) seem particularly upset that they have to pay bank fees here. They are used to free checking. My bank fee is around $10 per month. If I need a teller for something, I may have to pay a fee. If I want to take out more than €400 from my bank in a single day, I go to the ATM, print out the equivalent of a counter check/receipt for the amount I want, then take it to the teller who will complete the transaction at no extra charge. You can buy insurance through your bank. I'm good with that. I probably pay a little more per month than if I went through an independent broker, but the convenience of not having to navigate insurance (something that is hard enough to do in English) was worth it to me. For the record, my health insurance premium, with no deductible and an add-on dental plan, was about $150 a month for the first two years. It was over $900 a month (with a $3,500 deductible) in the US. An extra $5 or so doesn't faze me in the least.

You won't find some of the things that are readily available in the US. I now use PiriPiri instead of Louisiana Hot Sauce for my chicken wings. I buy my bread fresh from the bakery next door. Eggs aren't refrigerated. There is shelf-stable milk and cream. If you like yogurt, Portugal is nirvana. I'm in a smaller town so, while the grocery stores have some prepared foods, you don't get the buffet of ready-to-eat foods here that you do in the States. I'm okay with that.

You won't find bottles of Ibuprofen and other over-the-counter medications on the shelves. You go to the pharmacy or the pharmacist at the grocery store and ask. Ibuprofen here comes in 200 mg and 400 mg doses. If you have an issue, ask your pharmacist for a recommendation. They are extremely knowledgeable and could save you a trip to the doctor's—or advise you to get your butt to the clinic straightaway!

Be Okay with Not Knowing

I think this is the hardest one, especially if you're used to being the one in charge and having your life under control. ***Everything*** is confusing when you first arrive, especially if, like me, you don't speak the language. It's like going to a new restaurant: Do you seat yourself or is there a hostess? Do you pay at the table or pay a cashier? Where are the restrooms? Will the food be any good?

Now imagine everything you encounter is like that first restaurant visit. But the second time you go to that restaurant, you know to wait for the hostess and you know to pay the server. It's easier. My favorite little bakery is noisy and confusing, especially in the mornings when they are busy. Now I know when I walk in that it will be noisy and confusing. I also know the ladies who sit at the back table and we wave and say *bom dia*! I know the gentleman who sits with his laptop. And the guy with the bicycle who likes to stand at the counter and drink his coffee. Now the noise is normal to me because I know to expect it.

Every appliance you use has little symbols on it that you will need to figure out. (Yep. Google helps.) Apparently, my microwave also grills. (I still haven't used that option yet.) The washing machines have approximately 947 different cycles that you can choose from. (I found the one that works for me and I'm sticking with it.) I have a touch-screen stove top and I know what degree Celsius I need to set the oven at to bake brownies.

It's okay not to know something. Everything is going to take more time than you thought. You're going to make mistakes. Apologize and ask for help. Most people are really nice. (They might laugh at you later, privately, but they will help you.) Thank them profusely. The first words you should learn are "Thank you," "I'm sorry," "Excuse me," and "Do you speak English?" Good manners, a smile, humility, and a friendly (but not overly-friendly) attitude will work in your favor.

Here's the good news: The stuff that felt so weird and foreign when you first got here eventually becomes so normal you forget that it ever felt weird. I now look for the little ticket machine when I go in somewhere. I know not to look in the refrigerator section for eggs. I understand that I have to turn the water on close to full force to trigger the tankless hot water heater.

Courage is Often Just Fear in Motion

A lot of fear comes from not knowing what will come next. Two years of living through a pandemic has probably helped you become more familiar with daily uncertainty, whether you wanted that growth experience or not.

I had wanted to live in Europe all of my adult life. I wanted to experience it as a resident, not as a tourist. I wanted to see the places I had only read about or seen in movies. It was definitely a bucket list item. I worked on cruise ships when I was in my thirties and I saw people who *finally* got to take their dream cruise not being able to enjoy it fully. People would literally have strokes and heart attacks from the late nights, increased activity, rich food, and flowing alcohol. They weren't physically able to fully participate and enjoy this (expensive) once-in-a-lifetime experience.

The years passed and I saw friends starting to slow down. I started to slow down. People my age were hitting physical walls: cancer, diabetes, pacemakers, and yes, dying. My time for adventuring was running out.

It turns out you don't have to be brave to move abroad. I was more afraid of dying without seeing Europe than I was of moving. So maybe you just need to be more afraid of *NOT* doing something than doing it.

I'm not particularly brave. I am definitely not good with new things. I don't like change. I'm an introvert. Yet I picked up my entire life and moved it 4,000 miles away to a country I had never been to, filled with people who speak a language I don't understand. In spite of all this, in spite of me being me, I have never been more content. You don't have to be brave to move abroad. You can always go home again, no matter what Thomas Wolfe says. But if this is something you have always wanted to do, know that you can do this. People do it every day. Why not you?

About the Author

Barbara Grassey is a writer and expat, living in the Algarve, Portugal. She has written over 60 books, manuals and home study courses in the past 20 years for national speakers, new speakers, and small business owners. Her book coaching and publishing business allows her to work from anywhere in the world with Wi-Fi. She is very happy she landed in Portugal.

When she's not writing, Barbara spends her time taking walks along the Ria Formosa and petting all the good doggos (Spoiler Alert: They're **ALL** good doggos), having coffee or wine with friends, and feeling guilty about not writing.

Follow her expat adventures at My Expat Golden Girl Life:

https://barbaragrassey.substack.com/p/welcome-to-my-expat-golden-girl-life

You can also find her online at https://barbaragrassey.com/

Resources

An assortment of resources for you:

- Find me on **Substack**: My Expat Golden Girl Life. https://barbaragrassey.substack.com/

- My **business** website: https://barbaragrassey.com/

- **AIMA (formerly SEF):** https://aima.gov.pt/pt/viver

- **VFS Global**: https://www.vfsglobal.com/

- **US Embassy in Lisbon**: https://pt.usembassy.gov/

- **Americans & FriendsPT:** https://www.facebook.com/groups/505958149761247

Affiliate Links*:

- **Wise**: https://wise.com/invite/spu/barbarag424

- **Bordr**: https://www.bordr.io/nif?via=barbaragrassey

- **NIFOnline**: https://nifonline.pt/

- **GetSortd**: https://getsortd.idevaffiliate.com/idevaff iliate.php?id=103&url=7

- **Anchorless**: https://anchorless.io/?via=barbara

*If you click a link and purchase something, I receive a small commission at no extra cost to you. I will use the money frivolously. Thank you!

General Information:

- **Tax Treaties:** https://www.taxesforexpats.com/expa t-tax-advice/us-tax-treaties.html

Apartment and Home Rentals/Sales:
- **Idealista**: https://www.idealista.pt/

- **Olx: https://www.olx.pt/**

- **Long Lets:** https://www.algarvelonglets.com/

- **Places to Live for Digital Nomads:** https://bydigi talnomads.com/best-cities-for-digital-nomads

Shipping Companies:

- **Portugalia Sales:** http://www.portugalia.com/get_a_quote2.php

- **UPackWeShip:** https://www.upack.com/

- **Maersk:** https://www.maersk.com/ (Click on "Transportation Services")